T0244982

INTO THE SHADOWS, I RAN

I RAN

MY ESCAPE FROM POL POT'S COMMUNIST CAMBODIA

A TRUE STORY BY

THA CHHAY & MATTHEW RAUDSEPP

Into the Shadows, I Ran

©2023,Tha Chhay & Matthew Raudsepp

ISBN: 979-8-35093-457-1
ISBN eBook: 979-8-35093-458-8

TABLE OF CONTENTS

PROLOGUE

"When the Elephants Fight, it is the Grass that Suffers!"

AFRICAN PROVERB

DISTANT BOOMS AND A NEW HOPE

Cambodia, January 11, 1979 (Southeast Asia)

The Khmer Rouge holocaust ended quickly, just as it began. Early on January 11th, we began to hear what sounded like explosions in the distance. Distant booms sent birds in the nearby jungle flying in swarms into the early morning sky high above the tall coconut trees on the rice field's edge where we worked. That morning, hundreds of us, with our straw hats shielding us from the intense sunlight, walked among the tall rice grass, cutting and carrying the grass for harvest. Throughout the morning, the rumblings became louder. At times, I stopped my work to look toward the jungle and across the wide expanse of fields to discover the source of the sound. What horrors were the Khmer Rouge committing this time? We had no idea what was happening, and none of us in the village could have anticipated the events that would take place later that day.

1

Just before the arid afternoon sun reached its zenith, two objects out of nowhere whistled overhead until landing in giant explosions on the edge of the field, one on a large Khmer home that overlooked the field and the other in the dry field, spraying the red earth in all directions. The ground shook, as small sediment from the explosion landed around me. Yet it was not enough to move me from the field, where I continued to work on in shock. The imaginary shackles kept my bare feet immovable from the dry, cracked ground. Others around me did the same, immovable from their work, daring only enough to look up at one another with wonder in their eyes. Should we run for cover and risk harsh discipline from our longtime captors, or do we stay and wait—wait for the final breath that so many of our relatives and friends had taken in the past three years, eight months, and twenty days.

The Khmer Rouge soldiers ran out to the field, shouting for us to go into the jungle with them. They yelled, "We are one village. We must stay together and fight." Some of the workers, not knowing what to do and still in great fear of our longtime captors, followed them off into the jungle. The rest of us ran toward the village. We ran there because that is where others ran. We did not know who was bombing the field and the village. My aunt, uncle, cousins, and I lay flat on the ground near our huts.

From the nearby highway, tanks unloaded a volley of artillery fire into the field and the large Khmer homes in the village in an attempt to drive away the Khmer Rouge soldiers. After nearly an hour, the shooting stopped. The Khmer Rouge were gone. The eighty or so of us who remained, slowly got up. Some grabbed white hand towels or anything else that could be found of white material to waive at the troops. We ran toward them, not knowing who they were, or if they were going to shoot us too, but anyone who scared away the Khmer Rouge was more likely to be friend than foe. The soldiers were horrified by our emaciated appearance. Most people in the village were in their twenties and thirties, yet many looked like old men and women. The Vietnamese and Heng Samrin Cambodian soldiers welcomed us and offered us food. After we were given food, we were told to return to where we came from.

It did not seem real, as if it were a trick or a very vivid dream. I could not believe this to be true. Suddenly the realization occurred to me that, "Yes. I was free." It took an hour for this idea to fully sink into my mind. The Khmer Rouge were no longer in power, and we were free to leave. We were no longer condemned to live in the controlled village life that we had come to accept. The blackness that had hampered our spirits was suddenly brushed aside. Our black clothes no longer mirrored our despair. We no longer even had to wear the tattered black clothes, but that was all there was to wear. On Highway 5, Aunt Oiy's family and I retraced the steps that we had taken almost four long years before, back to our homes in Sisophon, in northwestern Cambodia. I was thirteen years old at the time.

Along the road ahead of us, our last remnants of disbelief vanished as we came across the bleeding bodies of recently killed Khmer Rouge soldiers. I think I recognized one of the bleeding men, a soldier who ordered a friend of mine to follow him into the jungle. My friend never returned, but I did see this soldier again often enough, ordering us around or reprimanding someone for some petty, slight infraction. We had to walk on the old, dilapidated highway with caution, as we could still be recaptured by soldiers hiding in the vicinity of the highway. A great heaviness fell off my shoulders, and I actually felt lighter. The years of waiting, surviving, and hoping had come to an end. Our toils had meaning, other than that of day-to-day survival for food. My family did not suffer the hardships in vain. There was now hope, like never before, that I would be reunited with my whole family once again. I kept looking over my shoulder, expecting someone to spring up onto the roadside from a hidden place behind bushes or scattered trees.

My aunt, uncle, cousins, and I headed back toward Sisophon. It took us nearly two days of walking, as we were exhausted and had not had much food for months. I parted from them on the outskirts of the city, as we took different roads to return home. Continuing down the highway alone, I began to feel unfamiliar with the surroundings. The many changes I perceived around me did not seem possible. I was filled with a sense of urgency to quickly reach my old home, to once again be part of the vague and distant dream in my heart. At first, I disregarded the differences all around me, but I soon realized that the small temples and attractive, large homes on the edge of town were no longer there. Yet the hills were in their familiar place. I could not have lost my way as I traveled along this road so many times in my childhood. When I finally reached my father's land, I knew that I was in the right place. I recognized my family's mango and coconut trees. But to my astonishment, my boyhood home was completely torn down. Nothing remained, except for a piece of the kitchen floorboard which laid on the ground near the base of a large tamarind tree. Even the small, sacred spirit house, on the corner of where our house once stood, where my mother's ashes had been kept, was completely smashed. Bits and pieces of wood lay scattered about the area where it once stood, including a tip of the small Garuda-winged roofline.

As I observed the scene, the shock of the unreal filled my mind, and the pit of my stomach churned in despair. Terror and the deepest depths of loneliness and pain crowded out my thoughts until rationality slowly returned. I was hungry, fearful of what had become of my father, brother, and sisters. A feeling so deep from within cried out. I could not name it. I fell to the ground, sitting on the place where my pet chicks and ducks had once played, years ago, beneath the place where my boyhood home once stood . I felt a sense of safety being on my father's land, yet suddenly the tears came and flooded my face with such extreme anguish and pain that I astonished myself, having been numb for so long to the tragedy that encompassed me back in the village. *Where was my family?*

After dispelling some of my pain and regaining my level-headedness, I decided that I had better find some food, and I started to look around to see if I could recognize anyone. I did not see any familiar faces. In wandering around the area, I found an abandoned warehouse where stacks of rice were kept. As I was one of the first few back, I found some giant bags of rice left behind by the fleeing Khmer Rouge soldiers. Being too small and skinny to lift the bags, I punctured them and filled up some thin metal buckets that I had found. I balanced the pails on a pole as I carried the rice back to my family's land. I went back and forth like this for some time, guessing that food in the weeks ahead would be scarce and very expensive.

With my heart centered on hope—hope that I would see my whole family again someday, as I had hoped each day in the village—I built a small make-shift hut on my family's land. I could barely stand the idea of my father, stepmother, sisters, and brother not returning. Days passed, turning into a week and then two weeks. I had my food now, consisting of the rice and fish from the nearby river, but no family. I was thankful to at least know that my aunt's family had survived. Where were my father, stepmother, and brother and sisters? Where did they go? Were they safe? I could not believe that I was to be left alone. At night, I frequently had nightmares, memories of horrific scenes I had witnessed. In my dreams, I played with childhood friends whose whereabouts I no longer knew, or I sat in a circle with my family having a meal, sharing laughter over friendly conversations. I reminisced about the earlier days of my pet cow and dog on the farm. I would wake up sweating, in complete darkness, lonely and fearful. The nighttime frog sounds would sometimes stop completely, and there would be complete silence, except for the sudden and intermittent bird call in the early morning, from an Asian koel (cuckoo), that would bring me back to reality.

During my wait there, I tidied up the area of my family home and fished in the nearby river to keep myself busy. One day nearly a week later, I recognized a former neighbor who had lived a street down from where our family's home once stood. And then, after two weeks of waiting, some-one came to my makeshift home. When I recognized him, I realized it was my brother, Vuutey. I saw a very frail, thin man, haggard from the work he was made to do by the Khmer Rouge soldiers. At first, I was uncertain who this was. When I did recognize him, I began to cry uncontrollably in relief. Vuutey could barely recognize me as well. I was now four years older than when he had last seen me, and I was still very meager looking from my life in the village. Excitement and elation were apparent in his eyes. When his bountiful smile broadened across his face, his dark brown-black eyes flashed a spark of indigo as they brought in additional light from the late morning sun. My brother laughed and cried at the same time because I was crying so terribly. He asked me, "Where is everybody?" And I said that I did not know and that I had come back with Aunt Oiy and Uncle Druin. I told him that I lived with their family these past two years after escaping from the other village where our father, Lem, and Gah were living. Aunt Oiy's family home was apparently destroyed, as our own had been. It was not visible on the hill, from where we stood on our property. I had been so distraught that I had not noticed until that time. I was in a state of shock with a type of tunnel vision. We talked for several hours, exchanging horrific stories of what we had survived. I was so glad to see Vuutey, but I was sad to learn that his wife had disappeared after being separated from him on the first day of the forced exodus from Sisophon. He had not heard from her since that day. Together we made a bigger shelter to live in, and he stayed with me for a couple of days before setting out to find our father.

The following ten days were grueling. I did not want to lose my brother just after having been reunited. I was afraid that he would return with no news or bad news. I spent those days just looking around the devastated city. I gathered wood and looked for more rice, and food. I also looked at others closely to see if I could recognize anyone. I did not wander far from my property, as I did not want to miss a relative who might come back. I had no worry of someone moving into my make-shift shelter because there was more property around than people. Many people never returned, leaving many places vacant.

When I returned from the river with some fish I had caught, I nearly dropped them when I spotted my brother on the land, standing near my father, who looked so old and withered. With them were my stepmother, Lem, and my younger sister, Gah (Lye Lye). I ran to them, hugging them—so joyful to see them. I was the happiest I had ever been in my life to see them again. We stayed up that whole night talking. It seemed so incredible that we were all together again. My father had only learned, shortly before the Vietnamese had taken over, that I was alive and that I had been living in the village nearby. He did not know whether I had perished or not two years before when I fled the camp for its lack of food. I could never get information about them from villagers in the nearby camp. It was as if they had disappeared. After I ran away through the cornfields that one afternoon, as I was starving and needed to find food, my father, Lem, and Gah were relocated to another village, not far away. To instill fear in others from doing the same, the Khmer Rouge soldiers made it appear that those families that were left behind by "runners," would suffer severe consequences. No one ever knew if a relocation was a move, or an extermination.

It was also fortunate that my brother had set out to find my father, stepmother, and younger sister, as only one day later, after they left their village, the Khmer Rouge returned and massacred everyone who was left behind. After the Vietnamese soldiers moved through, no one remained to protect those who stayed behind in the villages. Some people were afraid to go anywhere, since it was unknown where the fighting was taking place. We were joyous to see each other after such a long and terrible episode in our lives. The next day, we began to rebuild our home. I slept well for the first time in many months that night.

Later, my other sisters and distant relatives came. The bad news also arrived. We learned that one of my dad's brothers, his wife, and all of their children, six in all, were among those who were rounded up and most likely buried in the mass graves scattered throughout Cambodia. We still could not entirely believe that the stories of mass graves were true. It just seemed to be too staggering to believe. Also, on my mother's side, almost everyone was taken away. My uncle was a former military man, and so his entire family was slated for the body landfills. My Uncle Check was also killed as the Khmer Rouge had no patience for sign language, and my uncle could not understand their orders. It was very sad. My stepmother's sister, who could not be found on the day of the evacuation, never returned.

My brother's wife also did not return. It was another few years before we learned that she was still alive. During the evacuation from Sisophon, she became separated from my brother in the crowds. She was sent to work at a village not far from the Thai border. During the night, in a group of fifteen, she attempted to sneak across the border. She was one of the three who made it, while the rest had been shot during their attempt. The United Nations arranged sponsorship for her later in Paris from a refugee camp in Thailand, where she eventually remarried.

About a month after being reunited with my family, my brother and I decided to go to a nearby temple, Wat Chom Gah Kanol, just outside of Sisophon. We heard from others in the city that the once beautiful temple had been destroyed and that there were graves everywhere. This Buddhist temple, in my childhood, was among the most beautiful in the region. It had been situated on the lower slope of a hill. A trail that stretched one kilometer from Highway 5 had been neatly cared for by the priests of the temple. In my early boyhood, a stone border edged along the pathway to the golden, blue, and pink-colored temple in an opening in the jungle. A huge, ancient banyan tree had grown up over parts of the temple, providing welcome shade in the summertime before the war. Flowers used to bloom along the entire length of the walkway and in the temple's yards.

When my brother and I reached the temple, we were not prepared for the horrors that we found. The entire temple had been smashed, including large portions of the stone fence along the pathway. A few flowers remained, but what also remained staggered the imagination. Before even reaching the temple, we could smell a putrid odor, a portend of what we would find. We almost had to turn back before reaching the main site, as the smell was so awful. I vomited as the scene came into view of clothes and bones scattered everywhere. A portion of the temple had been dug up and filled in. Thousands of bodies remained, scattered over the temple site. Birds and wild dogs still feasted on the carrion that remained. Flies buzzed incessantly, everywhere. Yet the air was possibly poisonous for even wild dogs, so the bodies remained above ground, rotting. A large well three meters in diameter and approximately twenty meters deep that used to supply the temple with water was filled to the top with bodies. We had heard in the city that this is what had become of the temple, but we had to see it to believe it. And still today,

I can envision the grotesque and inhumane sights of that day. It was a place of evil that hosted angry ghosts—a place we had to leave immediately before being taken hostage by an evil spirit. Despite feeling so wearied after all that we had witnessed in the past four years, we quickly got back to the highway. The smell was the worst possible smell imaginable, and it took me a couple of kilometers of walking to stop heaving at the thought of what we had just seen.

The complete horror of the genocide was not really known or believed by anyone. All in the shadows of peace, among the largest countries of the world, after the Vietnam War had ended, this tiny war-torn country of Cambodia lost a total of 2,000,000 people. These estimates were not made until much later.[1] Despite the fact that my brother, Vuutey, had attended college, and both he and my father worked for the government, we were all spared, with a great deal of luck. My father wrote down "FARMER" on the ledger after we were all relocated, and my stepmother, Lem, had buried all of our family photos showing our better than average way of life, as my father owned a prosperous farm. No pictures remained from my early life. I am glad that my father made that choice not to be showy or grandiose, staying humble. My father gave the impression to the soldiers that we were just simple people, farmers with little education. I wonder how he knew, or how he found out, what we should do when it came time to declaring our jobs and family history to the camp leaders. During the forced mass exodus from the cities, there was a lot of speculation at night about what would become of us, or if the bombers were going to light up the areas we were camping. Word must have passed about how people were lined up and killed if they admitted to having any kind of formal education. My father did many good things for many people throughout his life and he possibly learned from those contacts he randomly met during the chaos on the roadway out of the city as to what should be revealed about our past to our future captors.

The Khmer Rouge, in their attempt to destroy the old culture, rounded up all of the educated people and their families in cities and exterminated them. Some were sent to "re-education" camps like Tuol Sleng, where they

1 Shawcross, *The Quality of Mercy*, p. 331.

were tortured before being killed. All the vestiges of my city, Sisophon, had been destroyed. Phnom Penh, the capital city, lost many citizens to the Tuol Sleng facility, which became a museum, a former school turned torture chamber. The devastation was so complete that it was like an evil experiment, to create Cambodia into a slave state of China, under the dictatorship of Pol Pot and his false philosophy, in an experiment that not only failed but brought death and so much pain and suffering to so many. It was an attempt to follow a new ideology, similar to Lenin's or Stalin's. We had no idea of the extent of the killings and destruction throughout the country, and it remained fairly hidden from the rest of the world as well. The distaste for the Vietnam War which spilled into Cambodia after all the bombings that were done by American B-52s along the Cambodian–Vietnamese border were kept mostly out of the media or knowledge of the American people for years. These bombings were used to play into "The Big Lie" by Pol Pot, the dictator of the Khmer Rouge, to say that Americans were on their way to bomb the cities. Nothing was further from the truth, as the war in Vietnam had ended, and the power vacuum was filled in Cambodia by the evil Pol Pot Regime. Our King Sihanouk had long since fled up into China, where he stayed in a type of house arrest. When we were finally freed from the Khmer Rouge encampment, we knew we were free from that horrible village life, but it was hard to release the shackles that had been implanted in our minds. There was no structure or guidance, just our fight to stay alive, and we did not know what way of life lay ahead for us.

Life for us was a great gift, as we were among the very lucky half of the population in Cambodia that had survived the Khmer Rouge holocaust. So much had happened to us, and so many worse things could have befallen us. Life was precious. We were fortunate to have each other. We had our early life memories, and we had our future. Yet many struggles still remained . . .

1

MY EARLY LIFE IN CAMBODIA

When I was a boy of four, I used to get up early every morning to help my sister sweep the walkway in front of our house. My sister Met and I always shared the same shoes, having only the one pair between us. My brother and sisters often shared everything, as my father could earn just enough to support our large family. Despite this, we did have many happy times in our home, playing childhood games during the daytime and dancing and singing with the entire family in the late evenings. I often got up on the table after dinner to dance for everyone. My mother said to me, "Tha (Tah), I will give you some more candy, if you dance for us tonight." While my mother sang, I danced and enjoyed watching my shadow on the wall, mimicking the shadow puppets of the *Reamker*.

My mother used to walk to the market every morning, dressed in one of her many beautiful, flower-patterned sarongs. From the vantage point of our porch, my sister Met and I waited for our mother's return. Although many of the streets were paved, cars were still a rarity in my hometown. We could spot Mother in the distance, walking softly along the roadway in her sandals, smiling at the neighbors and passersby on bicycles. Upon her return, she always greeted us with some candy from the market.

It was on one of these playful mornings, so early in my life, that events began to unfold in many darker and challenging ways. It was at this early age of four that one of the most significant events of my early childhood occurred. The day did not start out in any way unusual, as I remember it. In fact, it was quite a beautiful morning. The cows were basking in the morning sun, waving their tails at the flies. My sister and I were sitting on the porch, eating the candy that our mother had already given us. In the courtyard below, our mother swayed back and forth, singing to my aunt's baby daughter in her arms.

As my sister and I sat on our usual look-out perch, a commotion caught our attention from the street below. A strange dog was growling and threatening passersby. The dog tried to bite people who were walking down the street or who were riding through on bicycles. My sister and I looked on in dismay as the mangy dog began to walk in the direction of our courtyard. The dog, after spying my mother with the baby in her arms, began to pick up its pace and run toward our mother. Mom was too busy singing to the baby to notice the stray dog. "Mom! Mom! The dog is going to bite you!" we screamed. Before my mother thought to react, the dog leaped up, clutching its teeth into my mother's left arm. The dog growled ferociously, clenching its jaw deep into her skin. My mom cried out in pain, while trying to get the stray dog off of her. At the same time, she kept the baby in her other arm, as far away from the dog as she could. My sister and I started screaming, "Someone help my mom!" Our neighbor, after hearing the sound of our screams and the noises from the dog, grabbed a metal gardening rod, while getting the attention of my uncle. He yelled as he ran toward my mother, and he was able to use the metal rod to open the dog's jaw. It was very dangerous for everyone, as the dog could be rabid. Others also came to help, but by that time, the dog already lay motionless on the ground after having been struck dead by the neighbor's rod. He had to do it, as the dog may have been rabid. I felt weak and fearful when I saw the pain in my mother's face. Why did the dog bite my mom? My playful, smiling mother was crying. The bleeding was bad, and I could tell that my mother was badly hurt. I cried because she was crying—and I only vaguely remember today, my uncle and neighbor quickly taking her off to the nearest doctor in the area.

My mother returned later that day bandaged on her arm, and after having had to undergo a series of shots, my mother needed to rest. I was so relieved that my mother had returned home, but I could tell that she was not really well, and the cheerful happy glow in her personality was mostly absent. My father and eldest sister guided her to her room. My mother did smile when she saw me and then focused on going to her room to sleep. While my mother rested over the next three weeks, with the prescribed treatment from the doctor, my sisters took care of the home, with the cooking and cleaning. Our home, in Sisophon, in the northwest corner of Cambodia, consisted of a small one-story house raised up on twelve-foot-high stilts, that had a narrow staircase leading up onto the first floor platform. The house was just that one-story platform on stilts, consisting of five rooms in all: three bedrooms, a living room, and a kitchen. The floors were made from a thick, hard wood. As I had three sisters, the floors were constantly kept clean, polished so clean that I could see the shadow reflection of my face on the floor. We would use rice mats for sitting and sleeping. As is the custom in Cambodia, we never wore our shoes or sandals inside the house. During the rainy season when the Tonle Sap grew and the rivers leading in and out of it swelled, the area around our home became surrounded with water. During that time of the year, we would simply open a floor board up in the kitchen floor and fish directly through the floor. We would pull the fish right up into the kitchen. We would travel to neighboring homes, also built on high stilts, by wooden row boats. Yet this season was dry and very hot, so nothing like that was happening at that time. We just needed to ensure that our mother stayed cool while she recuperated. During the mornings, my mother was helped down to a make-shift hut that my father built, near our underground bunker, a necessity from the growing war to the east. My father with my elder brother, Vuutey, had built it in the previous years, and improved on it year-by-year. It was built on the highest point on my father's land in an area where the high waters never reached, so it could be useable year-round if needed. Many families with land near us created these as well, but I never really thought about it, except as a place to run to when we heard the military planes fly overhead. Most of the time I played carefree on the farm, or in our house, with my pet chicks and cow, "Onlong."

My mother had always kept the house spotless. The house was bare of furniture, except for a table in the living room and a small dresser in my sisters' room, for their clothes. My elder brother, Vuutey, and I would sleep, not in our own room, but usually in the living room. As it was always hot year-round, we did not need blankets, just pillows and rice mats. Usually after the evening singing and dancing in our house, I would lie down to sleep wherever I felt comfortable—no one cared, as I was a young boy at the time.

During this time, my father was home more often in the daytime, which I liked. I did not understand the potential severity of the dog bite, as I was too young. But I was old enough to be worried, and I wanted my mother to get well so that she could play with me. My mother stayed in her room, resting on her rice mat and pillow. We had electricity at our house. A small fan circulated the air around her room. In the first few days after the attack, she was still talkative, but more quiet than normal, and she slept a great deal. It took my mother two weeks of rest to recover from the rabid dog bite. She seemed to be much better after that time, but she was not yet back to normal.

These early memories for me were strange. To add to these unusual memories of my mother recovering from the dog bite, there was the somber daily reality of military aircraft flying overhead more and more often. In the morning, the planes would fly toward the war in the southeast, and in the evening, they would return flying northwest over my father's land toward neighboring Thailand. These were not typical planes, but the very large and loud bombers, the American B-52s. For the most part, life was peaceful in the northwest corner of Cambodia, where my hometown of Sisophon was situated. Except for these fly-overs of American B-52s, and OV-10 Broncos, as well as large helicopters that we would occasionally see, we would otherwise forget about the war raging on the eastern side of my native country of Cambodia. Our King Sihanouk granted permission to the Americans to bomb along the Cambodian border areas where the Vietcong were supposedly hiding. Unfortunately, the bombings became more frequent and insidious, as more and more of the countryside was getting targeted for these bombings. Sihanouk became increasingly unpopular as a result. News reports were spreading of huge swaths of land being destroyed, with Nepalm and that many villages along the southeastern border being shot up by OV-10 Bronco planes. It was becoming a concern for my father and my uncle as news spread of many innocent civilians getting killed. We did not know for how long this would continue, or if the war would begin to spread closer to us.

My father's underground bunker was getting used more frequently, as the fly-overs of various war planes made us feel uneasy. When we first heard B-52s approaching, we could feel the ground beginning to vibrate, and then really beginning to shake from their immense power as they got closer. The sound would get increasingly strong until the large B-52 airplanes would suddenly appear overhead, usually in a combination of two or three. We would run from the fields, or from the house, to this shelter that my father had made. It was more difficult to get to it when the flood waters were everywhere, so sometimes we would just freeze in place instead. We just never knew what these planes were going to do, but they did not do anything in Sisophon. They normally bombed near Kampong Chhnang, and the outskirt areas of Phnom Penh, as well as all along the Vietnamese border. My elder sisters, brother, and mother would quickly scurry down the dirt slope into the underground bunker when the B-52s could be felt with their approaching large engines. It was a unique sound that could be felt rather than heard. My father would rarely go completely into the bunker, but he would keep his head outside, waiting at the entrance of the bunker to watch and see where the planes traveled. My brother, Vuutey, and my eldest sister, Pah, would help guide my mother down there while she was recovering from the dog bite.

These times were increasingly strange. My father made a temporary hut using coconut fronds and bamboo supports, near the entrance of the bunker, for my mother to stay during the recovery from her dog bite, as our house with stilts and narrow staircase made it too difficult to get my mother from the house to the bunker. They would just arrive into the slope leading down into the bunker, just as the large planes were directly overhead. It was too dangerous, to take that long to get to the bunker. I remember the panic that happened each time when the vibration began to be felt, and we all rushed from wherever we were on my father's land to the bunker.

It became nearly a daily occurrence. It was disruptive to my playtime on the farm, but I liked being near my family so I didn't mind sitting closely down in the underground shelter with them. Once we were down in the shelter, we would sit tightly together underground, until we heard the vibrations subside, hoping that the planes would soon pass.

Our cows would become accustomed to the loud vibrations from the fly-overs, unless there were more than five bombers at a time. In most cases, they just looked up and swatted the flies with their tales, while we all ran for cover. But when there were many planes at a time, doing the fly-overs, they would get stirred up and start moving around.

It was the OV-10 Bronco airplane that really created fear in me. These planes had gunners in their underbelly. Also, I worried about the helicopters when they flew lower than normal. Occasionally, the large transport helicopters would open their doors, from where soldiers could peer out to the fields below. They could obviously see us, as we could see them. They normally reserved their ammunition for the eastern portion of the country, but they would occasionally be granted permission to fire on any village where there were reports of heavy Khmer Rouge or Vietcong activity. We were told not to move if we spotted the OV-10 Bronco fighter planes, as there were news reports on the radio and newspapers that these planes were instructed to shoot at anything that moved on the ground, although these instructions were reserved for the other side of the country, 300 kilometers away. We did not know what they would do. Being a very young boy, I would get so scared that I would begin to shake all over, and I did not move from the place I stood, when I spotted these planes every so often. I worried about the whereabouts of my father, brother, and sisters when I saw these planes. I did not want to get shot, or feel the pain of it, and I did not want anyone in my family to get hurt either. Amazingly, for the most part, we continued our happy life on the farm and tried to forget about the war raging on the other side of Cambodia. We just hoped it would soon end. I could not understand who all these different groups were that were fighting, and from where. We just wanted them to go away.

During the harvest season, about two months or so after my mother's dog bite, my mother insisted that she was well enough to continue with our plans to go to the rice fields about thirty kilometers away, to a place where my family owned a large field of land. It was time to harvest the rice. My mother, my elder brother, Vuutey, my three elder sisters—Pah, Paht, and Met, my Uncle Check, and I made the day-long journey together. My father stayed behind to work at his position for the local government in Sisophon. Gah, my baby sister, stayed with Aunt Oiy, my father's sister. Once there, we made a camp, preparing to live out of a small hut on the edge of the rice paddies for a couple of weeks while harvesting the rice. There wasn't a bunker built there, so we would just freeze in place when military planes flew overhead. They would not normally shoot at farmers, and in our part of the country. Yet we just never knew. There was a deep pond near the property that we could run to, if we needed to go into the water to hide, but we did not have to go there.

During the first full day that we were there, everyone besides my mother worked in the field, including me, although I was only four. Actually, I spent most of the morning chasing small butterflies and making games with pet insects that I found. My mom stayed behind in the camp, as she still needed to rest. It was also her duty to prepare our meals. The day was extremely hot. After a few hours, I wanted to go back to the camp. I also wanted to see how my mother was doing. In some way, I sensed that something was wrong, so I asked Vuutey if I could go back to see Mom. He and my eldest sister, Pah, did not want me to walk back by myself, because I was too young, and they did not want me to wander off by myself. But finally,

Vuutey agreed to let me go. I think he was more irritated by my persistent begging, so he relented. So off I went.

After getting back to the small hut, I noticed that my mother was lying on the ground. At first, I thought that she had lain down to relax. I called out, "Mom? What are you doing?" Then I looked into her eyes, and I saw that they were very red.

"I am feeling sick," she said. She kept spitting the water out of her mouth.

I kept saying, "Mom! Mom! Get up! Get up!"

She then told me "not to come too close to mommy, because mommy is getting kind of confused. Mommy might hurt you!" Then she told me that I must go get my brother and sisters, to take her back home. I was in shock. She told me again that I must hurry. I was wondering how I could just then run back to get my brother and sisters. It was not a short distance back, and I was already a little out of breath. I did not want to leave my mother alone. I turned around and ran back toward the field, running and crying, wanting to get back to them, using all of my strength. When we finally got back to the camp, we found our mom lying on the ground. With a great deal of slurring, she could only whisper to Vuutey to take her home.

We put up the camp and went home right away. We did not have a car or anything, just a bullock cart pulled by our cows. We put our mother on the bullock cart to let the cows pull her home, while we walked along-side. She was feeling worse and worse, as we made our way back home. We were all very worried. When we got home, we sent for a doctor to come to our house. She started saying that she was very sick and did not feel that she would live very much longer. She kept saying, in a very soft whisper, to my elder brother and sisters, "You take care of your younger brother and sister, because Mom is not going to live longer. And don't hurt each other." She asked one of our neighbor's sons, who was about the same age as my eldest sister, Pah, "Can you marry my daughter?" He was happy to agree. His mother was a close friend of my mother, a sweet neighborly lady, who was frequently in our home, and she was also there now to comfort her. This was on the first day back, at about 2:00 a.m.

On the second day, her condition became unbelievably worse. She did not recognize anybody, nor could she eat anything or drink water. She was getting weaker and weaker. I was worried about her, but I could not believe that she would not be with me anymore—her playful dancing, the morning candy, and her wonderful smile. I was her favorite, being her youngest son, and being her favorite, I would not let her go away. On the third day, it was not likely that she would improve, so a Buddhist priest from the nearby temple came to our home and prayed for her until about 9:00 p.m. That evening, Met and I, along with my baby sister, Gah, were taken to my Uncle Druin's and Aunt Oiy's house, nearby, because we were too young to be allowed to witness the final rites for my mother. Aunt Oiy told Met and me stories to get our minds off our mother. I was very upset, and I just wanted to go back to see my mom. Unfortunately, my wish was not to be fulfilled. She passed away that night, around midnight, to the shock of everyone, as she was still fairly young, at forty-two years of age.

The next day, my mother's body was taken to the place where the body would be burned, as was the custom. In Cambodian culture, children are not allowed to see the dead body of their parents, but I asked my dad if I could see my mom's body anyway. My dad agreed, but I could see her only for a few minutes. When the few minutes passed by, they tried to take me away, but I refused to go away from my mother's body. They kept pulling my hands back and forth. They did not want me to stay there any longer. Finally, I relented and went back to my home. My father's stepsister, my Aunt Gil, comforted me, held me, and told me that I would be fine, until I fell asleep.

2

AFTER MY MOTHER'S DEATH

My mother's death left a deep void in our family. We were all grief stricken at the loss, and my father, a widower with six children, had added responsibilities. My father, Jaik, was a strong man, both physically and in character. He was popular in our community and was even well-regarded for his decision-making, at the nearby temple. Although he was forty-seven, he was still quite strong and able to manage the farm while continuing to work for the government. He had the uncanny ability to smile, even when he was angry. It was difficult to know when he was upset. Only one time, when I was eight, do I remember him ever getting angry with me. He asked me to look after the cows while he was away, but instead I decided to play in the river with a friend. When he came home, he did not see me or the cows anywhere, until he spotted a few of the cows eating in a neighbor's yard. From the river, I could hear him yelling for me. I got a good spanking for that. Most of our cows were black, and so were those of our neighbors, so it was next to impossible to determine which cows were ours. That was the only time that I saw my father angry. He was a gentle man with a very good heart, a strong will, and a determination to get projects on the farm done. I admire him, and I loved his company.

There were several women who showed an interest in my father when my mother passed away. None of them really interested me at all. The woman he chose as his new girlfriend did not work out well. Luckily that relationship lasted for only a few months. I was pleased to see her go as she did not show that much warmth toward me, and was not much fun. As my father was considered a very handsome man, there was soon another woman of interest in his life. Her name was Lem. Soon after, he took her as his wife in a small ceremony, in the Cambodian tradition. Lem was tall for a Cambodian woman and very pretty. She caught onto my liking of candy, and we became friends. But more than that, in the challenges that were awaiting us, she became crucial to our family's survival. My stepmother, a sharp-minded, attractive, and loving woman, was very good to my brother, sisters, and me, taking care of us as if we were her own children. She had only one daughter of her own, and that daughter was older than my oldest sister and was already married and lived in another village.

I continued on with my chores despite the tremendous heartache I felt, as I still missed my mother so much. In the early morning hours, I would often get up to wait for the ducks to lay their eggs. I would collect some of the eggs for our family to eat. We also had chickens. I used to take care of the baby chicks, of which there were more than a hundred living under the house. We would sell them when they matured. There was a garden in the back that extended into our farm. Banana trees, mango trees, and sugarcane fields were all neatly separated from each other in rows. We had sixteen to eighteen cows that were all used for harvesting the rice and towing heavy materials on the farm. As our farm animals always actively took part in our family outings, it seemed as if they were a part of our family too. I had my favorite cow. His name was Onlong. The Sisophon River ran its course not more than two hundred meters from the back of our house. Once a year, in late September or early October, the flood waters would rise, flooding many areas along the river, including most of our land. The mud would get so sticky, in the days before the flooding, that it would make it almost too difficult to lift our feet off the ground, as each step added more mud to our shoes. The soil was almost black from the rich nutrients in the soil, most likely a result of the annual flooding. The land that my father owned had been in my family for several generations. During most of the year, it was such a beautiful and convenient place to live, that my father improvised by building a house there, several feet above the ground on strong, wooden stilts. During the period of high waters, the chicken and ducks that made their home under our house had to be taken to my aunt's house, on higher ground. All of the chicks had to be caught and put into bamboo cages. They, along with other animals on the farm, were transported on bullock carts pulled by our cows to my Aunt Oiy's house, two kilometers away.

The flood waters actually marked a fun time of the year for us, a time that we always looked forward to each year. When the water deepened, we would use a wooden row boat, large enough to carry six of us at a time with supplies, to travel to wherever we needed to go from our house. We could also fish from our front porch or through the kitchen floor during this three-week period. We knew many of our neighbors as we would share necessary things and sometimes would travel on the boats together to the dry land to walk to the market. In the kitchen of our home, a section of the floor which pulled up allowed us to catch fish swimming beneath the house. During most of the year, this small opening was used for feeding scraps to the chickens under the house. But this time of the year, my mother, and later my stepmother, could fish directly from the kitchen, through that opening. My mother was excellent at catching fish this way. She would drop a string into the water with a hook attached to the end. She would use tiny shrimp for fish bait. She would also throw rice in the water to attract the fish. In Cambodia "dreygrine" more commonly known as the small, wide Thai fish, could be easily caught under the house this way. From the front porch, my brother, Vuutey, and I would catch catfish, about ten to twenty centimeters long, along with "dreygrine" and "dresah" another kind of fish that looks like a white trout or a four-inch long tilapia.

Some of the neighbors that had houses built closer to the ground were sometimes flooded out during the wet season. The flooding was not that bad along the Sisophon River unlike the annual flooding along the Tonle Sap. On the edges of the large lake, which is similar to a miniature ocean, people would live in floating huts or houseboats year-round. They would be anchored to the ground by rope. The houses would rise and fall with the floods. Each summer, the ropes would be checked and resecured to make sure that their houses did not float out into the great lake. Not many people lived in stationery, low-lying homes because everything would be washed away each year. Some people did, and during those two to three weeks, they made it a traditional practice to live with their neighbors on boats, constructed just for the flooding period. The temperature was still very hot, and the water made everything even more humid, but it was not as hot as the very arid part of the dry season in the months of March, April, and early May. The low-level lightning storms that filled the sky with brilliant colors each afternoon during the beginning of the rainy season were also less prevalent at this time. One year, a neighbor lady, Las, was caught in the corn fields, when a lightning storm broke out. From the distance, another neighbor witnessed a lightning bolt, so sudden and seemingly from nowhere, strike her down. It was very dangerous to be out in the late afternoon, when the storms began to blow in each day from the southwest. But as the rainy season moved into full swing, the flood waters actually marked a pleasant and fun time on our land, though just stickier and more humid than usual—a small price to pay for so much splashing fun.

My relatives were mostly farmers, aside from my father. Vuutey attended the university, outside of his chores on the farm. After he graduated, he worked in the customs department, where he would check cargo carried by trucks or on the trains that came through Sisophon station. Our land provided us with most of our food. Each morning, we ate a breakfast of rice soup and fresh fruit from our own banana and mango trees. Orange juice was also common, but we did not have orange trees on our land because they could not last through the annual floods. The oranges came from my Aunt Oiy's land on a nearby hill. My mother, and later my stepmother, always worked so hard to take care of six children and my mother's disabled brother, my Uncle Check, who was mute and deaf. I have cheerful memories of my mother working away in the kitchen, with a warm, friendly smile, making sure that everyone had something to eat. Uncle Check seemed like an older brother to me. The same age as my oldest sister, Pah, he worked alongside my father and brother on the farm. My uncle, despite his sensory disabilities, got along just fine. My mother always looked after him with the same kind respect that she gave everyone. It was very fortunate that my stepmother, Lem, continued in my mother's footsteps to take care of everyone. In the years that were to follow, my family truly became indebted to Lem's unselfish diligence, which I believe greatly enhanced our chances of survival.

I still miss my biological mother. Throughout my life, I have often reflected on the happy times that I shared with my mother during my very early years, and I was glad in a way that from her premature death, she was protected from the horrors that would befall my native Cambodia in the years to follow. Or perhaps, she was there alongside me, in spirit, during those very difficult and trying moments, to watch over me as a protector. Even today, I wonder about that.

3

FORCED EVACUATION
FROM THE CITIES

It was five years after my father's marriage to Lem that the Khmer Rouge, a militant communist faction, sponsored in part by Mao Zedong's China and the deposed King Sihanouk's government, began to terrorize the cities and villages throughout Cambodia. It began gradually in the early 1970s with thieving and roadblocks, amid other growing political troubles, crescendoing to their eventual takeover. In 1975, in a matter of days, the whole country was swept into their control. Anyone who was remotely involved with the Lon Nol government or who espoused the old way of life, contrary to the Maoist precepts of the Khmer Rouge (Red Khmer), were taken away, or had simply disappeared. Even King Sihanouk was betrayed by the Khmer Rouge and put under house arrest at his palace. A few lucky people were able to flee to neighboring Thailand.

Immediately on the day of the takeover, announcements were made on the radio that everyone living in the cities must leave for the countryside by the next day for fear of bombing raids, supposedly by American B-52s. Only that night was there any time for preparation, and everyone assumed that they would have all of the next day to ready themselves for leaving. Just after sunrise, the ground shook and dust-laden air blew inside our home, as military trucks blazed by on the street outside. My sisters and I peered out at the developing chaos. Shouts blared from big speakers attached to combat vehicles. The Khmer Rouge soldiers, dressed all in black, except for their insignia of red and white checkered "kramas" tied around their necks and faces, moved like black beetles over their trucks and from house to house. Waving their machine guns in the faces of our neighbors, they commanded everyone to leave at once and to follow Highway 5 eastward into the countryside. They told everyone to be out of the city by noon. We were told to take only a few belongings, as we would be allowed to return in three days. On the radio, proclamations were also made, telling everyone to leave the cities.

The scent of Vuutey's clove cigarettes began to fill the air in our house, as he nervously lit up. In much the same way, the insidious smell of terror was also beginning to fill the air of our once happy and comfortable home. Everyone had to pack and go immediately. Pol Pot's communist revolutionaries, the Khmer Rouge, were in complete control of the country. The bulletin from the radio went on to say that any refusal to leave would defy the government's official edict, and death was the punishment for disobedience. All the cities in Cambodia were being evacuated. Only the Khmer Rouge were allowed to stay. Panic ensued.

My father decided that my stepmother, my three youngest sisters, and I would stay together. Vuutey and Pah, my eldest sister, would go with their spouses in different directions, splitting up. My Uncle Check went with Pah and her husband, Hey. Vuutey and his wife, Heng, traveled in their own direction. My father thought it was best for us to separate. There was fear that people involved in the old government, even at the lower levels, would be killed along with their families. My father decided that we would bring three of the cows, a small amount of gold, approximately forty grams, along with a small stockpile of food, a few items of clothing, and a plastic tarp for cover. Of the animals remaining on the farm, Pah and her husband, with Uncle Check, took three cows, and Vuutey and his wife, two cows.

Everywhere people took to the streets. Everyone was confused and did not understand what was happening. My father did not have any real plan yet, only that we must stay together with the cows and not let each other out of our sight. As everyone was being sent eastward, my father hoped that we would be able to stay at a friend's village in that direction. Hysteria swept over the city as people packed what they could. Parents were forced to leave children behind, as they had not returned to their homes by noon. By late morning, Khmer Rouge soldiers began going house to house killing the residents inside who did not move out of their homes fast enough, putting their bodies along the roadside. It created a frightening hysteria, and we were not sure who these soldiers were, or if they were really part of the new government. Although, my father knew the area east of Sisophon well, it did not matter during the first day, as all 50,000 residents streamed out of the city in a giant river of people. We said goodbye to our happy home, with its chicks, ducks, pigs, and mango trees. All I could think about was my family being split apart and about how much I would miss my brother and eldest sister. I was also sad to say goodbye to my cows and chicks.

We felt very strange leaving everything behind. All around us people walked. Everyone was watching everyone else, not sure what would befall us. The road was too narrow for all the people, and everyone walked, pressing against each other, as they followed the stream of people in front. People were nudging from behind, saying, "Faster! Faster!" There were reports of soldiers, at the back end of the crowds, threatening people with their guns and bamboo sticks, pushing people onward, faster. No one wanted to wind up at the end. I was scared that I would become separated from my parents and sisters. I stayed close to them. Lem walked behind us, to make sure that we were not separated in the crowds. My father took up the front with the cows. All around us, people stepped on each other's feet. Animals pressed against people. Children who were forced away from their parents in the crowd were screaming and crying out for their mothers. Eventually, people spread outward to the front and to the back as far as one could see. And no one knew for sure how far they were from the trailing side of the crowd.

One small boy walked alongside us for most of the day. He would sometimes be ahead of us, and at other times, he would fall behind us. Everyone watched as he screamed and cried out for his parents. When it began to get dark, a family adopted him so that he would have a family to stay with that night. Parents were screaming out the names of their lost children. People who were forced to leave behind loved ones were crying everywhere. Families were forced to be split apart. My little sister, Gah, about five years old, cried as people nudged her on both sides, almost crushing her at times. The weight of the belongings that we carried made our bodies ache, but we moved on in fear. In the extremely crowded exodus, it took six hours to cover only four or five kilometers on that first day. Movement was hampered by the dense crowds of people.

We followed Highway 5 out of the city, which led its way toward Battambang and eventually Phnom Penh, 370 kilometers away. Our family walked until the afternoon with the vast crowds, not having any plan of where to stay, or of where or what to eat. We did not have time to bring anything else. We were fortunate to be together, as many families were split apart. My stepmother could not find her sister before leaving, and she was very worried about her, but there was nothing that she could do to help her.

At about 3:00 p.m., we stopped for a rest and for a short meal of rice. At about 4:00 p.m., all over Cambodia, rain fell in torrents. With nowhere to go for shelter, we walked for some time in the rain until we stopped in the middle of a rice field for the night. We covered ourselves with the blue plastic tarp, except for my father who stayed out in the rain. Lem sat halfway under the blue plastic tarp, enabling my three sisters and myself to have complete cover from the heavy rain. Very few families brought any type of plastic coverings, or any type of tarp, so many huddled under what trees there were, which was actually dangerous for the possibility of sudden lightning strikes. Thousands of people stayed in the rice field with us that night. Each group watched other people, with uncertainty in their faces. With wood that we found, we made a small fire to cook some fish and rice. My father looked apprehensive and very sad, sensing that his old life was gone, and feeling uncertain about where to go and what would happen next. We were all thankful for his foresight in bringing the plastic tarp with us. That night, we talked amongst each other, about the things left behind and what lay on the road before us. I was never able to see my chicks or my boyhood home again. My father let all the animals loose before leaving them behind. We did not know where they went, as they did not know where we went. I was nine years old at the time.

The next day, we again walked, this time a longer distance, about eight kilometers. It was a very sad day, although it was easier to walk. Beside the road, many elderly and overweight people died from exhaustion. There were personal items scattered everywhere along the road. Lem was getting tired from carrying Gah, who was having a hard time with the long walk. The walk was not far, but it was slow moving, requiring us to stand for many hours on our feet carrying all our belongings that we brought with us. Gah was still so small and slight that my father feared she would be lost in the crowds, or get stepped on by an animal, or wind up lost, unable to force her way forward to get back to the family again. My father could not carry her as he had to maneuver the cows through the crowds. Despite Lem's strength, Gah was becoming too much for her to carry. But, at last, we finally reached the village of Honokutrey, the village of my father's friend.

As Honokutrey was very small, it was still intact. No one was required to leave small villages in the countryside. Upon reaching the home of my father's friend, we learned that several of his relatives had already taken refuge in his home. My father's friend offered to let my two sisters, Paht and Met, stay in his home, but they refused. They were afraid to be separated from the rest of us. So we resorted to making a camp on the ground, in the village. We were not alone in our decision to wait there, as several hundred other families also chose to stop there. We simply slept on the ground and cooked food from our supplies.

We had enough rice and dried fish to stay in the village for at least three weeks, if necessary. My father thought we ought to stay in the village, without traveling any farther, as we would possibly be allowed to return to the city. He did not want to risk any of us getting separated again. But in the days that followed, we learned that people who had tried to return after the three-day period were killed. There was nothing to do in the village except sit and wait. There were no stores or any basic comforts. We just had each other.

My father spent as little gold as he could, trying to save the gold and watches, which he had also brought, for possible later use. Others who brought only bags of money were soon disillusioned. At first, the money was still useable, but it was practically worthless. Food items began to cost ten times their normal price with currency, but with gold, the price of items only inflated by about twice their original price. Eventually the *reil*, the Cambodian currency of the time, became worthless, and it would never again regain any value. In the future, a different currency was printed.

After two weeks, the Khmer Rouge took control of the village, making a list of everyone there. Everyone had to register their name. Each person was asked to write down their former occupation. If someone had been part of the military, he was required to write down his military number. My father wrote down only that he was a farmer, with no mention of working for the local government in Sisophon. Some people were more than eager to write down "soldier," and their number, in hopes of getting better treatment for their families, and more food rationings. People who admitted to having university degrees, and those who had military experience or previous government affiliations, were loaded up in buses with their families and "relocated" to other villages. We had a foreboding sense about those "relocations," and we later learned that they had been taken to the newly arranged body landfills not far from the village. We were also not aware of the cruelty of the various killings that were going on, until much later. Buses would stop alongside a newly dug landfill, and one by one, the passengers in these relocations would get off the bus. A soldier, with a two-by-four, would strike the person in the back of the neck, killing the person instantly, in most cases, or knocking the person unconscious. The body would then fall forward into the landfill onto the pile of bodies below, as people watched from the windows of the bus and waited their turn.

4

THE ENVELOPING DARKNESS: THE KHMER ROUGE VILLAGE

A supreme supervisor, or governor per se, took control of our village. The *Rem*, as he was called in Cambodia, had complete control of everything. He kept tight control of the camp, with his group of fifteen to twenty Khmer soldiers who walked around with their guns monitoring everyone's activities. They never worked in the fields, as they only gave orders and rendered discipline. All six hundred people in the village were divided into groups of ten. Within each group, one supervisor was selected. The person had to be between fifteen and thirty years of age, no older, but sometimes much younger. He or she would watch over us, making sure that we did not say anything bad about the village or the work. Amazingly, many of these camp supervisors were trained children. Some were as young as ten years of age, just a year older than me. I believe they were recruited as they were too young to truly understand what they were doing to others. Possibly, their parents out of hope to direct attention away from themselves and their children, may have encouraged it. Unfortunately, some of these young recruits were instructed to kill people as well. It was hard to understand really, but no one could trust anyone outside their family. Young recruits would go under family huts at night and listen for negative conversations directed toward the Khmer Rouge and report these families. Rarely were people over thirty years old recruited to be a supervisor within each group. The supervisor was to ensure that everyone worked during the day and that the schedule was maintained. The supervisor role was not necessarily a sought-after position, as the Khmer Rouge soldiers did not discriminate between anyone and would punish whoever they felt like punishing when a problem occurred. At first, those who were selected felt that they would be able to use their influence to improve their own family's situation, but in most cases, it was better to remain "unseen" as much as possible, otherwise they would become known by name to the Khmer soldiers. People were put in groups of ten, and put together by age. I was in a group of other young children, and one of the soldiers would select a group leader for the ten in a group. The nine other people in the group would monitor the supervisor, to make sure the supervisor stayed in line as well. My father and Lem joined another couple, along with some single men to make up their group. After working during the day, I was able to stay with my father and family for a couple of hours, but later I had to return to my group of ten children for the night. We were all given a strict working schedule each day. We were to stay in the village and to never leave. Everyone was given black clothes to wear. All other clothes were to be handed over to be dyed. Anyone wearing any color other than black would be punished—so it was without question, on that day, that the whole country of Cambodia was literally shrouded in darkness, turning to the color of black.

Each day, we were told again and again that we were not to run to Thailand, which was fifty kilometers away. We were never allowed to talk with people in other units, aside from our immediate family, but it could never be with disparaging words toward the Khmer Rouge soldiers or our work. During work, if we worked alongside other units, we were not allowed to communicate with them in any way. Also, we were not allowed to talk amongst ourselves. Despite these strict rules, news still spread, when the soldiers were not present. Information would be shared that people had successfully made it across the border to Thailand and were immediately assisted by the United Nations to go to America, Canada, Australia, or France. Information from other villages would also be shared in this way. Occasionally, two units from separate villages would be working alongside one another in the rice fields or doing other agriculture projects. Opportunities would arise where information could be exchanged. It was through this way that we eventually learned that Aunt Oiy was living in a village nearby.

During the first month, we continued to sleep on the ground, until huts were constructed. The huts only had poles holding up a roof made of coconut palms. The roof protected us from the sun and rain. During windy rainstorms, we would put a blanket up on the side where the rain was blowing in to keep the ground of the hut from turning to mud. It was a year before walls were constructed. In the four years of village life, we never had electricity. My dad's friend was forced out of his large house to allow the Khmer soldiers to live there instead. Our village, made up of many huts, faced west across a large field of rice paddies. Trees to the east blocked the view of sunrise, which I never saw during my time in the village. We began work in partial darkness, working until the sunset could be seen beyond the fields to the west. We were only offered a short break once a day, if there was food to eat.

At night, we had to be careful while talking, as a group of spies, or, in Cambodian, *gong chehlope*, developed. Made up of boys and girls about my age, they were willing to take easier jobs in exchange for spying on neighbor families or their own. No one could mention anything about their life before 1975—Year Zero. Complaining was not allowed. We often worked without food for several days. Dancing and singing were forbidden. Families that were overheard talking about such things were taken away during the night, never to be heard from again.

In the cooking halls and in the fields, one could hear the Khmer soldiers bragging about their last kill, about "how their hand felt so good after the last one," or "how easy this one was to kill." One of the single boys in our unit lived separately from his family, yet when his family had been taken away, they eventually located him too. We were working alongside each other in the rice field one day, carrying the rice grass to be planted, when a Khmer soldier came up to him, telling the boy to go with him. He was to join his family in a "relocation." He said goodbye to me in such a way that I could not mistake the real meaning that was there, that I would never see him again. While continuing with my work, I glanced in the direction of the soldier and my friend to see where the soldier was taking him. After the soldier walked my friend two hundred meters away, far enough away to where no one would likely see them, the soldier bound his arms behind him before taking him back to the camp to be loaded on a truck to be taken away. We were not allowed to cry or express our feelings, because it was the rule. With sadness, I still remember that day so clearly in my mind. It was difficult after working alongside him for almost a year.

Our schedule started at 5:00 a.m. every morning. Generally, we would work all day for twelve to fifteen hours, and if there was food, there was an hour's break for lunch or dinner. At the beginning of the day, our supervisor would get the assignment from the master schedule of where we would work that day. We had to work in the field no matter what the conditions were, whether it was heavy rain or extreme heat, with just our straw hats for protection from the hot sun on our faces. Everyone had to work in the rice fields or had to grow vegetables. Some groups also fished, and others, who were lucky, worked in one of the two kitchens. In the first year, before extremely rigid control was mandated, we ate in our huts with our own family, but later, after having had to give up our pots, spoons, and other personal items, we were forced to eat only in one of the two cooking halls near our huts. About ten people each worked in both kitchens. We were only allowed to eat with others in our group. The kitchen workers would have to bring food out to us in the fields if we were too far out to eat with the rest of the village. When there was food, we usually ate rice soup with a small chunk of beef, chicken, or pork, about two centimeter square. However, we often did not get to eat anything. We sometimes went for entire two weeks without food, forced to live off water lily, crabs, or fish that we furtively brought back with us to our small hut in late evenings. During the wet season, when the rice fields flooded in knee-deep water in some places, fish from the neighboring waterway would make their way to the field where we could sometimes catch them.

During these times, when food was not delivered to our village by the Khmer Rouge soldiers, the kitchen workers also had to work in units out in the field. My father was skinny and very deteriorated-looking after being so strong and robust on the farm, back in Sisophon. Sisophon was another life, and our old lives, as time moved on, became increasingly distant for us in our minds.

Often while I worked, I wondered why everything had happened the way it did. Deep down inside, I felt that this would all come to pass, in some way, somehow. I just focused on getting food, any little bit that I could get. I was too weary from fear and malnourishment to spend too much time thinking. I hoped that I would see my family again. I missed my elder brother and sister. My life had to change. Maybe I would somehow get out to Thailand and be done with this miserable existence. Everything in my life was the village, the rice field, and the discipline. We all worked for free, without even being fed, day after day. For me, there was no school, no Buddha, no market, no food—nothing. It was forced imprisonment, for nothing more than being born Cambodian. Deep down, I believed that I would not be killed, and I just hoped that the country would change. But at the present time, the whole country got up early, went to bed late—there was fear, work, and very little food. I could only hope that one day I would see my whole family again, somewhere, some way.

To hide what few items we still had, Lem would get up early, before everyone, to bury family pictures and other items, wrapped inside thick plastic, in out-of-the-way places around the village. She would do this before others would wake up, and in the evening, when no one was around, she would dig them up. This became her daily ritual. As my father and elder brother had worked for the local government in both Sisophon and Battambang, there were pictures of them dressed up in better clothes, better than what most people wore during the time prior to "Year Zero." If the Khmer soldiers were to ever find the pictures, they would have assumed that my father and elder brother were more educated than most and that they had worked for the government. Although my family had a better than average income for Sisophon, we were relatively poor as a result of our huge family size. Pictures of my brother, who graduated from the college in Sisophon, could also implicate all of us. My father did not try to talk to others for fear of divulging too much information about this life in Sisophon. The pictures that we had were all we had left to show of our life before 1975. But one day, we suffered a terrible loss. A rainstorm swept through the area, where a deluge of water flooded many areas. The sudden rain waters began to flood the fields. It was as if the heavens were attempting to wash away the evil that was permeating the soil. There was flooding everywhere. That evening, when Lem retrieved the pictures, only the paper remained. The photos had been ruined. And what dim colors that did remain had all but dissipated in the days that followed. The water had completely ruined the photographs. As a result, I do not have any photos of my early life or of my real mother—just a fond memory of her in my mind. I grieved over this for many weeks, but grieving was not uncommon as the blackness continued to envelop us.

During my second year there, I came down with malaria. I did not know what it was at the time. I would get the shakes uncontrollably and run a high fever. I was often weary, especially as I often did not get enough food to eat. At night, we were not protected from the mosquitoes that flourished in the wet rice fields. We could hear them buzzing in our ears all night. We were often so tired after working all day that, when we slept, we would occasionally put our arm outside the net or accidentally open up the small net a little, allowing mosquitoes to get to our skin. Most of the nets that we used were in poor shape, some having small tears in them so some mosquitoes could find their way inside the netting. As for malaria, the Khmer Rouge offered two kinds of treatment. One treatment was a made-up remedy of theirs, which to this day I believe to have been made only from the milk from young coconuts—this worthless remedy was to be ingested orally. The other method, which left me with scars, was an acid treatment with a mixture of their medicine, which they would apply with cotton presses to my stomach area and back. I still have three scars on my front and three on my back from this treatment. These scars have stayed with me as a daily reminder of my life in the village. Both methods were ineffective for me; however, the latter method did seem effective on others. Malaria was a constant battle for everyone. My father never caught it, but my younger sister, Gah, did. She had a mild case of it, and it lasted for, luckily, only two months. As for myself, my case lasted about a year. Constantly in fear of being taken away for being sick, I stoically continued to work. Another worker in our unit developed an acute case of the disease. He could not work for two weeks and would wake up in the middle of the night screaming and laughing. One night, he disappeared. In a few days, I happened to come across the remains of his bloated body in the woods near the village. It was likely if my symptoms became worse, I would suffer the same fate.

The somber life in the village continued on in much the same way for about two years. Our housing improved somewhat with the installation of walls and bamboo matting. The amenity of bamboo matting made for more comfort in our one-room hut. Unfortunately, the openings for windows, with no glass, made for easy entrance of mosquitoes, wind, and sometimes rain. Food rationings became desperately worse. My two elder sisters were eventually taken from us, and so from our family, it was just my father, stepmother, younger sister, and I who remained. All the boys and girls above fifteen years of age were taken away to other villages to be taught the doctrines about the new way of life. We were constantly harangued about our life in the village as being the "best way to live—the best kind of life." We sure as hell knew better than that!

Food became more and more scarce. Despite a large warehouse in the village that was full of food, it was not uncommon to go without food for more than a week at a time. In fact, in my second year there, it was difficult to believe that people in the camp were once healthy, normal looking people. I became shamefully aware of how skinny and bony my own body began to look. My knee caps and ankles were particularly visible. About seventy to eighty people in our village died from the lack of food. My malnutrition was so severe that I experienced a constant ringing in my ears. Among other dangers, poisonous snakes lived in the rice paddies, mainly cobras, that did not like being disturbed. Snake bites were rare, but occasionally someone would be bitten, and the Khmer Rouge did not offer an antidote to the snake venom. Death was almost immediately certain. However, more people died in our village from starvation, or that in combination with malaria, than from any other reason. By the end of my second year there, the number in our village shrank from six hundred to a little more than four hundred. Occasionally, people would sink down in the water, collapsing in the rice fields.

5

RUN, BOY, RUN!

On one of those occasions, when we went without real food for more than two weeks, I could not bear the hunger anymore. I decided to leave on my own, to seek out the neighboring village where I had heard my Aunt Oiy was living. I heard that in that village, a regular share of food was offered. I wanted to discover on my own whether this was true or not, and to see whether my aunt's family was still alive. If their food rationings were better, then I hoped to somehow blend into their village with my aunt's family. I may have been delusional from the lack of food, where I convinced myself that this would be a good idea.

After going a short distance away from the village, I found myself, suddenly in the midst of giant corn stalks, with ripe corn waiting to be picked. I reached up and took some corn, and being so hungry, I bit into it raw. I did not see anyone, and being so skinny and small, I figured that I would not be seen in the field. After just two small bites, someone grabbed me from behind. I had no idea that the soldiers were in the fields watching, as I did not see them anywhere until being grabbed. As I later learned, the fields were always closely watched when the crops were nearly ready to harvest, as so many desperate, starving people from around the area would take the food. The Khmer Rouge soldiers thought nothing of killing people for the slightest infraction.

Weary from hunger and too tired to run, I could not get away. Several of them were upon me at once, asking me where I had come from. I told them that I came from the neighboring village and that I was hungry. I was scared, but I did not care in a way because I thought that I would die soon of hunger anyway. Being Buddhist, I began to rationalize that I was not meant to live longer than my short eleven years in this lifetime. They bound my arms tightly behind me and took me back to my village. My father was told of my capture, and he immediately went to where I was being kept. The soldiers bound me up in front of a large mango tree in the center of the village. As they normally did before executing thieves, my captors proceeded to shave my head. My dad pleaded with the *Rem*, the commander of the village, saying, "The next time he steals, take my life instead. Do not kill him!" After scaring and threatening me, the soldiers left me there under the tree. I could not leave as I was all tied up. No one was allowed to talk to me. The sun was searing hot, but the soldiers said before leaving me, "We will not kill you this time." I stayed there, tied to the tree, wondering if they were really going to kill me or not, or just leave me to the elements. I really was dazed with hunger and fear. I really did not care anymore and began to become listless, although I did cry at times when my awareness would occasionally sharpen and my hope returned. Food did arrive in the kitchen that day, but I was not allowed to eat. Later that day, in the afternoon, my father went to see the *Rem* and pleaded for me to be released. Finally, at about four or five o'clock in the afternoon, they unbound my arms and let me go back to my family. My family cried, and they were relieved. I slept, although I was still painfully hungry.

In the days ahead, I was able to receive small quantities of food. However, I felt that I would not survive, if I could not get more food to eat. Two weeks later, I no longer cared about the punishments that I might receive. I left once again to go to my aunt's village in search of food. I could tolerate the hunger no more. I did not take anything from the fields this time. But instead, I unfortunately stumbled into a unit of workers from a neighboring village. I was asked to show my papers that gave me permission to walk from village to village. I told the soldiers that I was given permission to go to the neighboring village to see my aunt and that the *Rem* told me that papers were unnecessary. They threatened me, accusing me of being a "runner," and said that I had escaped from my village. They put me to work with the unit in the rice field until very late that night. Throughout the day, they continued to threaten me. I had to continually convince them that I would not run, and that I would eagerly stay there to get food for the day's work. That night, I had to sleep in the rice field as I did not have a hut to sleep in. That night, I knew that I had to devise a plan of escape. I thought, my days were numbered and they would finally get bored from yelling at me and kill me. It was too dangerous to run off in the dark, uncertain about which way to go. Being so tired after working all day, I would surely get lost. I would have to wait for the next chance to get away, which had to be very soon.

The next morning, I was forced to work alongside the same unit again. The same soldiers met up with our working crew again. I promised that I would not run off, as a Khmer soldier came over and yelled at me at a hand's length from my face, saying that I was "a worthless, rat runner." Everyone in the unit had gone without food for some time, as I did. We were not given any food on the previous day, but no one complained. The morning was dreary. I was filled with anxiety about needing to get away. It was just a matter of time before my use to them would wear out and they would find more fascination in watching me die. It was at lunch time, when food was finally offered that I realized that this would be the opportunity, possibly the last, for me to get away. No one paid any attention to me after the announcement that food rations would be allotted. Despite my severe hunger, I knew that this might be my only chance at escaping. It could be days before another opportunity would present itself, and they might kill me before then anyway. Fear and adrenaline welled up within me. I could barely wait until everyone walked away to the kitchen. At first, it appeared that a couple of soldiers were going to stay behind, to make sure that everyone stayed together, but at the last minute, they seemed to lose interest, walking away with everyone else. The leaders assumed that I would not pass over eating, so they did not notice when I staggered behind and ran into the jungle, when everyone else was running off to the cooking hall. So into the shadows, I ran. When I entered into the tree line near the edge of the field, I was certain that someone would jump out and grab me. It was now or never, and it seemed that I had actually gotten away. Almost in disbelief, I moved on. I had to find my aunt's village and stay out of sight. I walked through the rice fields in water that was as high as my neck at times, to hide from any other Khmer soldiers or from any other people in other villages. I moved as quickly as I could, afraid that before long, they would realize that I was missing and come after me. I had to be very careful, as I could not afford to have another delay or predicament in another village. My body was getting weary, and I had to hope that my luck would continue. My chances of finding my aunt's village were very uncertain. After moving through the rice fields and jungle for some time and getting far enough away that I felt that I was a safe distance from the last village, I began to slow down my pace. For a while, I was overcome with a sense of freedom, out in the middle of nowhere, away from all of the turmoil back in the villages. I began to reminisce about my home back in Sisophon, memories of my brother, sisters, mother, stepmother, and father—the old times, before the Khmer Rouge. I could not be tempted to feel this way for long, as all around me, there was danger. The knowledge of freedom for that time provided me with the energy to persist for another few hours through the fields and jungle. If I could not find my aunt's village, I would die. I had no idea whether I would be able to find it or not. Luckily, the area where we were kept by the Khmer Rouge was not far from the area where my family went to harvest rice each year, so I had an intuitive sense of the area. After six hours of walking through high water, farms of cotton bushes, and rice fields, I came across another village. I was tempted to stay low and go around it, but with fortuity, I spotted someone in the village who resembled my cousin. She was wearing a straw hat and black clothes, on the edge of a field of cotton bushes. She was cleaning and pruning the area under a row of cotton bushes. She happened to stand up just briefly and I could see the side of her face. I was wondering if I was tricking myself with hope. My hunger made me somewhat delusional, and I could not see as clearly as I normally could. I could barely believe it that I may have finally reached my aunt's village, after so much trekking. I carefully approached my cousin from the side of the field, asking her, "Are you Eep?" She was surprised and shocked at seeing a stranger on the side of the jungle. Then a different amazement came over her face when she recognized me and saw how much different I looked. She was so skinny that I could barely recognize her from her slight figure, but when I heard her voice, I knew for sure that it was her. She commented to me that I, too, looked very skinny and different. She pointed to her hut in the village. I carefully made my way there around the cotton bushes and waited there until she could get word to my aunt that I had sneaked into their village.

That evening, my aunt told the kitchen workers that she was not feeling well, so she would take her food and eat by herself in her hut; when she entered the hut, she reached out to hug me and tears welled up in her eyes. She could not understand where I came from. She quickly gave me more than half of her small meal of rice soup, just liquid rice with no meat. I quickly gulped down the portion, having gone so long without food. I could easily have eaten many times what she gave me, but I was happy to have been offered just half of her food.

Although I was beginning to feel quite tired, we talked quietly for quite some time while sitting on the floor of her shoddy bamboo structure. She was so happy to hear the news that my family in Honokutrey was still alive, but she was very concerned about their lack of food. I told her about the soldiers and the working unit that I ran into in the cornfields during my escape a few days ago, and about my decision to run again when everyone was distracted by the announcement of food. I told her about my first attempt to leave the village when I was caught, tied up, and brought back to the village, and my father's pleading for my life for taking two bites out of the raw cob of corn. I told her about my escape earlier that day and my efforts to stay hidden on my trek through the land, and my luck in recognizing Eep working on the side of the field of cotton shrubs. My aunt devised a plan, and with the risk of making myself known to the village, she decided that she would ask the *Rem* of her village if I could stay to work there. She felt that because she had rapport with him and that because she was able to sweet talk her way into other favors for her family, she would be able to persuade him to let me stay. I agreed and realized it was my only choice. With this plan, there were many risks for everyone. While she went to his house, I stayed behind in her hut, scared that they would want to kill me again. She was fortunately able to persuade him into letting me stay, but under the condition that I would have to work alongside the adults, doing the heavier work, not children's work anymore. She explained that I had fled from my village because all in my family were dead, and that I was desperately hoping to find her. It seemed that lying was a constant regimen for survival. So it was in this way that my stay with my father, stepmother, and younger sister in Honokutrey came to an end. There was no way they could know that I was safe, as no easy communication was allowed between villages. They could only have the hope that I was still alive.

I felt very lucky in finding my aunt and uncle. In retrospect it seemed that somehow I was divinely guided, because I would have surely perished had I not found their village that afternoon. In the following two years, I got to know my Aunt Oiy and Uncle Druin, who were among my favorite relatives. When I was much younger, I always enjoyed playing with my cousins, especially with their baby daughter, Eep, at their big home. Their daughter Eep and I were pals from a very early age. During the wet season back in Sisophon, my father would make me stay with my aunt and uncle each year when the flood waters peaked. Their house was on a much higher ground than ours, on the slope of a hill, and it was visible from our house, although it was more than a kilometer away. They had a wonderful large home, with large fields full of coconut trees. When I was very young, I was often excited to get coconut milk every day from my aunt when I stayed with her. On their land, they also grew orange trees, so I would also get to drink very fresh, sweet orange juice there. They kept a small hut on their land, just for our chickens, ducks, and pigs, for the wet season. Our cows also stayed with their cows during that time of the year, to avoid the high waters near the river. One year, my father made me stay there for a particularly long time because the waters were taking a long time to recede, and there was the possibility that the rising water would flood our home. The water came to just two centimeters below the floor of the house, when the water finally peaked. The waters stayed relatively high for more than a month, the worst flood that my father could ever remember. Luckily, the house survived, and the floors were not damaged. The wooden floors in our old home was made from a particular hard wood that did not warp or crack easily. It was very sturdy and of high quality so that it remained flat and did not warp, despite the damp waters underneath. Unfortunately, the sugarcane and rice grass did not fare as well, being submerged for so long. For two weeks, they would survive the flooding, but, after a month, when the water finally receded, there was nothing left. All the plants had washed away. This problem occurred in many areas throughout Cambodia, so that year, as rice shortage occurred, the rice, which is the main staple food for Cambodians, became very expensive. It was interesting to compare the problems of a few years earlier to those of the present time, as former troubles seemed so unimportant as compared to the present challenges that we all faced together. I was just thankful to still be alive, after surviving already so much, and I was also thankful I had discovered that more of my relatives were still alive.

I stayed with my aunt and uncle, working alongside them in the cotton fields and rice fields day after day. I missed my father, my stepmother, and my sisters and brother terribly. I also wondered about Uncle Check and my other relatives. I hoped that they would not starve and that wherever they were, they would be all right. I hoped that I would see them again. It was later that I learned that father, Lem, and Gah had been moved to another village, several kilometers away, after my escape. Letters were not allowed in Cambodia at that time. There was no way to communicate between relatives. I had no idea if my brother or my three elder sisters were still alive. However, I was fortunate that I was still younger than fifteen, the age when all the boys and girls were separated from their family. I had really no idea of where I would end up in case of a separation. Life seemed very uncertain and dismal. Yet,

I had my aunt and her family close by. And, for the time being, I had better food in this village, not a lot better, but more than before.

6

THE PSYCHOLOGY OF MY SURVIVAL AND MY NEW HOPE

My life was taking shape as that of an agrarian slave to the Khmer Rouge regime. We worked day after day, without ever having a break from the tedious work. Life was uncertain, weary, and joyless. Sometimes, in the village, I wondered if we would all disappear from the world without a trace, without anyone ever knowing about our plight, about our way of life, or about our early family life. In the many times when I felt that I was not meant to live a long life, I always believed that my own soul would somehow be protected from the evil that was all around me. But I did not focus on this, as my strongest motivation to stay alive sprang not from fear but from my deep desire to see my whole family again, all reunited back in Sisophon. I was filled with anger so much of the time, but there was nothing that I could do, out of fear of what might happen to me if I spoke or lashed out. And whom would I complain to? My love for my family motivated me to move forward, as well as the appreciation for my aunt and uncle's family provided with me a sense of duty and responsibility to continue on.

There was no suitable punishment that I am aware of that fully fits the crimes of the Khmer Rouge. A person cannot be brought back from the final sentence of death. A price could never fully be paid to make up for the years of separation from family. Abuses, tortures, and maiming cannot be turned around. Tears shed cannot be completely forgotten.

I felt very angry for being forced to leave my comfortable, happy life behind in Sisophon. I hated the Khmer Rouge for the separation from my brother and eldest sisters, and from having to leave my animals behind on the farm. I wanted to crush the Khmer Rouge, like one squishes an egg. I visualized this over and over again in my mind. The Khmer Rouge killed good people, and they did not care. For me, the Khmer Rouge were pure evil. They were the worst people imaginable, and I no longer even viewed them as even being human. How quickly they recruited young people for their cause. If it was fear, the desire for power, or betterment for their own family, I could only guess as to what persuaded them to join their ranks. I was often listless and just did my daily work without questioning it. I had no choice, and I did not have much energy to combat them, or to risk my life or my relatives' lives, by speaking out against them.

My father had explained to me how some people are born with the "evil blood," and during their lifetime, they lust for killing people and hurting others. Sometimes it is just for small, quick gains for themselves. If they cannot overcome their "evil blood" or bad Karma, then at the end of their life, their souls will be tormented with horrible rebirths, and they will continue to be reborn to experience horrible torments, sufferings, and agonies until at some point, they are rehabilitated and learn how to love and contribute to the happiness in the world. Because of this Buddhist philosophy, I wondered what I must have done in another lifetime to be having such a horrible experience of my own.

I just focused on working hard and trying to stay low in the village, out of the minds of the soldiers. I worked so hard to save myself time and time again. I was more fortunate than many, to still have my wise and clever

48

Aunt Oiy and Uncle Druin, as well as my cousins, to help me through the most difficult times. We all focused on helping each other. We shared whatever extra food we found, and looked after each other. It was the love for my family that made me want to live. Our nonverbal communication was quick and key to our survival. Sometimes it was just a look of warning, or a look to keep our heads low. Having this emotional support from my relatives, I felt, was key to my survival. I hoped that my father, Lem, and Gah were still alive, back at the other village. Many people "cracked" after experiencing so much trauma. Some people suffered severe amnesia, and they could not remember anything that had happened to them. They worked on in a robotic state in the fields. Other people went crazy after their loved ones were killed. Deep down, my cornerstone of sanity, which helped me to be strong, was my own fundamental sense that I wanted to survive, and I deeply felt something better would happen to me. I hoped to see my family again. It also helped me tremendously to know that most of my family had at least survived the first two years. For others in the village who were not as lucky to have this immediate family support, they just tried to survive themselves for the sake of their family and family's prior love for them, although many faced tremendous despair knowing that their loved ones had been killed.

In my Buddhist upbringing, I believed that if warmth and love emanated from a person, then warmth and love emanated back toward them. If evil, pain, and hate emanated from one's soul, then evil, hate, and pain emanated back toward them. In the case of the soldiers, with their hate and cruelty to their own people, this could not go on forever, but for how long? Nobody knew. I just hoped that someday, this would all change, and that a better life waited for me. I thought mostly about food, and about when I would next eat in a very driven way. When you don't eat for a week, you feel horrible. The focus was on food, water, and sleep. I longed for my family and to hear the laughter and playfulness of my sisters and brother.

My father was a lay Buddhist monk, which meant that he worked but participated in functions of the Buddhist temple. He could have his family and his own business and hold a regular job. He was a very spiritual man, very wise and practical. My father told me that when it comes to Karma, people will eventually go onto a heaven, to await being reborn, and then they continue their cycle of rebirths until reaching a high level of perfection in their spirt and soul, over thousands or even hundreds of thousands of lifetimes in this dimension and others, and that they move into a place called nirvana, a place of no rebirths but of eternal bliss and peace. Truly evil people, after they die, are reborn in torturous circumstances many times, and for the sake of everyone, and themselves, will hopefully be rehabilitated, freeing them to move into more positive karmic cycles. This was the part of the Buddhist philosophy that was ingrained into my mind by my father and some of the priests of Wat Swai at an early age.

As I was a young boy, all of this made me feel a little better, yet I was filled with so much hate and anger at times, that I just wanted to see the Khmer Rouge soldiers dead. If they were dead, I could be free to see my family again and have food to eat. I hoped that all of the Khmer Rouge soldiers would die, so that good Cambodian people could go free. But this was not the way for me, and I was powerless to do anything. I wanted to be able to trust others, but it was wiser and better to not trust anyone, except my aunt and uncle, and cousin Eep that I felt closest to. On one end, I was filled with hatred and anger, and on the other, I was filled with love and hope—together, these feelings created an energizing force for me that sustained me when there was no food to eat . . .

On the morning of Thursday, January 11, 1979, I was working alongside Aunt Oiy, Uncle Druin, and Eep in the rice field, among several others. Eep looked over to me, with an odd expression on her face, and she whispered, "Can you hear the strange noise?" I looked at her sadly without replying and then I also began to hear a strange sound to my amazement. It was like a pounding, or what sounded like distant explosions. When I made eye contact with her again, I nodded yes, while continuing to cut the rice grass. I also looked around to Aunt Oiy who had apparently heard the distant rumblings as well. With our eyes, we communicated perplexity to one another, having no idea what it meant. Was it an approaching storm of huge magnitude, although it was unlikely as it was not the rainy season? Or were the Khmer Rouge up to some other form of destruction? As the minutes dragged on, the sounds faded, and there was no sound other than the soft sound of birds chirping in the jungle nearby. Later in the morning, the soldiers were engaged in heavy conversation and activity near the Khmer Rouge homes. I did not stop to look, but they seemed unaware of all of us in the fields, for the first time that I could remember.

In the early afternoon, the sounds began again. Explosions could be clearly heard now. Maybe someone was fighting the Khmer Rouge. A battle of some kind was definitely brewing. None of us knew what to think, and we wondered what this would mean for us in the coming hours. Would we be rounded up and asked to leave the village that we had built, or would the fighting end before they reached our area. They were obviously getting much closer, whoever they were.

Suddenly, a whizzing sound echoed through the fields. People looked up briefly to find the source of the noise, before one of the Khmer homes suddenly exploded on the side of the field. Three or four other explosions sprayed red earth around the other houses still standing. Panic ensued, as people ran back toward their huts, and more whizzing sounds could be heard as shells pummeled through the air toward the Khmer Rouge encampment. Someone was fighting the Khmer Rouge. People shouted and some began pointing toward the narrow highway to where tanks and other miliary vehicles were moving along. We ran toward our huts, because that was where others ran, not knowing what to do or where to take cover.

Khmer Rouge soldiers came running into the field yelling at everyone to follow them into the jungle. Some soldiers grabbed whoever was close to them, pushing or throwing them in the direction they wanted people to move, in their anger. Out of fear, many went with them into the jungle. The Khmer Rouge soldiers yelled, "We are one village." "We must fight!" "We must stay together!" Aunt Oiy, Uncle Druin, Eep, and I all lay flat on the ground near our hut, not sure what to do. Instinctively, all of those around us did the same. We sure as hell were not going to fight to support the Khmer Rouge, and hopefully, we would not be forced to do so. We stayed low and silent. My eyes were tightly closed. The last image in my mind was seeing the backs of two Khmer Rouge soldiers as they disappeared into the jungle, while one huge blast, not far from where they entered the woods, destroyed a tall coconut tree. We stayed on the ground for some time, unsure about how much time had passed. Suddenly, everything became very quiet, and there was complete silence. Then the sound of the military vehicles moving again could be heard. I opened my eyes once again.

Some people got up and ran in the direction of the soldiers that had scared away the Khmer Rouge. Some had even found white cloth to waive. The vehicles stopped. Soldiers stood and stared at those who were first to reach them. Amazed at the sight of the emaciated figures standing before them, the soldiers greeted us. In our tattered black clothes, the first villagers to reach them got down on their knees and begged the soldiers not to harm them and thanked them for scaring away the Khmer Rouge. After seeing this, I began to run in their direction as well. Anyone who scared away the Khmer Rouge was more likely to be a friend than foe. Our liberators were kind to us, offering us food, and introduced themselves to us as Heng Samrin Cambodian soldiers, and Vietnamese. They told us that the area was now under their control and that we should all return to the cities that we came from. I could not believe it. After four long years, we were finally free to return home.

We did not linger long with the soldiers, and immediately, we set out to return to Sisophon. We were cautious on the first day of our return, staying in a rice field with hundreds of others that first night. Remembering my encounters two years earlier of units working outside the village, I was filled with trepidation. Maybe the soldiers had only taken over small areas, leaving other areas still occupied by Khmer Rouge soldiers. My Uncle Druin said that we should return home. So we traveled down Highway 5. Along the highway, we saw the bodies of recently killed Khmer soldiers. Our trek back home over the badly maintained highway took until the afternoon of the next day, before we finally reached the edge of Sisophon.

We separated on the outskirts of the city, as my family's home was on much lower ground, and they had to take travel up a hill to get to their old home. I was worried as I walked on alone, as many of the usual landmarks were gone. It was difficult to part from them, as we had been together through so much the past two years. I needed to see if my father, stepmother, and sisters and brother had returned yet. I continued to walk on, as I had done so many times in my dreams back in the Khmer Rouge village. Yet, so many of the homes or small temples along the highway were missing and everything seemed awry. Once I arrived back at my father's land, I knew that I was in the right place, as the coconut and mango trees were there, but to my astonishment, my boyhood home was completely gone. Not even the small garuda-winged spirit house that had been situated on the outside corner of our home remained, where my mother's ashes had been kept. Only a small piece of wood from the kitchen floor, the door that had swung open for feeding the chickens or catching fish under the house remained. The house had been demolished and burned to the ground. A feeling so deep from within cried out. I sat on the ground where my pet chicks and ducks had once played years ago, beneath the place where my boyhood home once stood. Then suddenly, the tears came and flooded my face with such extreme anguish and pain that I astonished myself, having been numb for so long to the tragedy that encompassed me. *Where was my family?*

In a few moments, I realized that I must find food right away and set out to find wood to make a make-shift shelter. I found rice at a nearby storage shed, and I carried several buckets full back to my father's land. That was a bonanza, a storage shed full of rice left behind by the fleeing Khmer Rouge. That was the most food I had for months. I found buckets to transport it in the shed as well, just within a short walk from my family's land. I was able to start a small fire to cook the rice with water from the nearby river. I had food now, actually a great deal of food with fish from the nearby river. I cooked the rice directly in the bucket itself as I did not have a pot or pan to cook it, but I did not care. First step was to feed myself, and then catch some fish, as there were many in the lazy river that I could see from the bank. I focused on catching fish so that when my family arrived, I had food to give to them. As I did in the village, I embraced the hope of seeing my whole family reunited again in the hours or days ahead.

Two weeks passed before I recognized anyone, and then to my surprise, my brother, Vuutey, arrived. I cried out in happiness when I recognized him. He could barely recognize me as I had grown so much since I had last seen him. I immediately offered him fish and rice. He could barely recognize me as I had grown so much since I had last seen him. I also looked so skinny, from being so malnourished. Vuutey looked much older than before. He looked thirty-five going on forty, not twenty-seven. After spending a day with me, he set out to find our father, Lem, and my sisters. Again, I waited for almost another two weeks, before anyone arrived. And then one day, as if heaven merged with earth, there they were, our father, Lem, Gah, and Vuutey, all back on my family's land. My father reached out and embraced me. He looked very old now, and Lem, quite weathered as well, squeezed me in a tight embrace. Gah, who was so skinny, was now nine years old. We rejoiced in being alive together. Father and Lem were not sure that I had survived my escape. It was not until Vuutey had told them, after finding them, that they learned for certain that I was still alive. In the days to follow, my elder sisters, Pah, Paht, and Met, also returned. It was truly the happiest time in my life to be reunited with my family once again.

Once the war ended, and I was reunited with many in my family, I began to relearn what happiness was all about, and, since then, I have strived to be happy and to enjoy the things that I liked doing in my life. Sometimes, just being alive, "just being," was the most wonderful thing, in itself. I began to cherish even the little things. I was glad to see people smile again and have food to eat. Just to be alive was a gift to be cherished—to be able to breathe in and out, and to smell the air. After seeing so much evil and injustice, I could only want to do good and be full of love. I wanted to live in a good place, where people could love each other and be happy, and not be filled with hate and the desire to kill. With this in mind, my family set out to rebuild our home, and to rebuild our community and our lives. I was thirteen.

7

MY LIFE AS A BOY MERCHANT IN CAMBODIA

In Sisophon, jobs were scarce, actually nonexistent. Lem made some money for our family by making clothes, cooking, and selling sweets. She sold food to many of the people who migrated through Sisophon, on Highway 5, toward the Thai border. In the weeks that followed our family reunion, hordes of people filled the highway leading out of the country. Many felt that it was best to attempt passage to Thailand with the hope of leaving all the troubles of their native, war-torn land behind. My father felt it was best to stay.

My father, Gah, Pah, and Paht began to farm again. Vuutey was able to get a position as a police officer for the new city government in Sisophon. With my friends in town, I started selling goods between cities with money that my brother gave me. After a few months of resettling, my brother raised about US$150, in gold which I used to get my business started. In Sisophon, I would buy merchandise which was brought from the cities of Aranyaprathet and Poipet in Thailand about thirty-five kilometers away. I took the rickety-old buses over the devastated roads up to Phnom Penh and sold items there, with my friends. Although I was thirteen at the time, I was treated as an adult. Everyone had gone through so much, and I needed to work to support my family.

I learned how to trade from an older friend in Sisophon. I traveled to Phnom Penh to see how he did his business in the daytime bazaars there. I began to do as he did, buying clothes, cigarettes, medicine, stereo equipment, and even bicycles, or whatever I believed would make a profit, and reselling them in Phnom Penh. I would have my goods loaded onto the top rack of a bus. Everyone's personal items on top would be covered by a large plastic tarp that provided protection from the rain and searing sun on the long bus rides. I would also put items under my seat or just carry them on my lap during the journey. I also used the train or the ship that went over the Tonle Sap, whichever my friends and I decided to take. I became quite familiar with many parts of Cambodia.

My friend in Sisophon introduced me to some of his friends in Phnom Penh. Soon, I became well-known among the others as the young merchant in the market, or "black boy," as I was sometimes called, as my skin was darker than that of most Cambodians. When I was in the capital city, I became particularly good friends with an older woman of thirty, Ain, who looked after me as if I were a younger brother. She had lost her husband during the holocaust, and she worked hard to raise her two kids by herself. I often stayed with her in her nice home. When she traveled down to Sisophon to buy from the market there, she would stay at my house. She always brought food, mainly fruits, as a gift for my father and my younger sister when she stayed with us. My father always appreciated the gifts and found my friends to be interesting guests, with their many stories and ideas of their own. When I went to Phnom Penh, I occasionally stayed with another friend, Succun, who became like an older brother to me. He was senior to me by eight years but respected my talents for negotiating and selling in the market. His father, who had been a professor, did not survive the war. I met both Ain and Succun while working alongside them in the daytime markets. The three of us became very close, and we often spent the late evenings at the nighttime market, drinking coffee, tea, fruit juices, or beer. I especially enjoyed the nighttime market, as everything was so lively with loud music and lights everywhere. My times with them were among the happiest of my adolescence.

I developed a finesse at trading goods, and I made several friends who would travel with me on my trips to different places in Cambodia. I never traveled alone. Several of us would travel together, doing the same business. Ahead of time, we planned out which articles we would buy, and we would also get other items that looked interesting enough to resell in Phnom Penh. One of the safest ways to travel was by ship, from Siem Reap, over the Tonle Sap. We would all load our goods onboard and spend the day talking and joking. The ship would dock in the pretty city of Kampong Chhnang, where we would spend the night. The town was well known for its many brick buildings. It was a nice town that seemed like a big garden in many respects, with giant trees and flowers. None of the brick buildings were over three or four stories in height. The market was right on the waterfront where our ship docked. The town's economy was based primarily on the fishing industry from the great Tonle Sap. We often ate inexpensive fresh water fish dishes with rice in the restaurants there. We slept on the boat on hammocks. Passage by ship cost about 150 Cambodian *new riels,* or less than US$2, at the time. This price included free food, but we usually bought other food on board the ship as well. The ferries were two-storied and fairly flat, with the only enclosed structures being indoor toilets and a place to purchase food. Each person had to bring their own light-weight hammock with them, to tie up along the walls of the boat if a person wanted to avoid sitting or lying on the floor during the long ride. With the hammock, a person could sleep on the boat, at night, when the ferry was in port. The journey consisted of two parts, with the nighttime stop-over in the port city of Kampong Chhnang, the midway point of the journey.

The Khmer Rouge never took to the water in boats, so there was never any worry about sniper fire from other boats on the Tonle Sap. However, they sometimes shot at ferries that traveled up and down the Mekong or Tonle Sap River, but I never witnessed this during the times that the ferry passed from Tonle Sap onto Tonle Sap River, for the last part of the voyage, to Phnom Penh. My only concern was torrential rainstorms, which I luckily never encountered while away from shore. Once out on the lake, the land would disappear in the distance. I wondered where I would go, if the ferry were to ever sink. Turbulent weather would also mean miserable sleeping conditions while docked.

On one passage by ship, I arrived only ten minutes before the departure from Kampong Chhnang with new merchandise that I had purchased. The usual cargo areas in the forward section of the ship were already full, so I went to some storage rooms in the aft section of the ship to find space for my additional belongings. As I was storing my wares in the room, I stepped on a tarp that I thought covered bags of rice. It was very strange footing, as if, at first, I had stepped on something soft that suddenly became more solid under my feet. It had to be someone hiding inside an open space between the rice sacks. I stepped back, surprised, as I thought that I was alone in the room. I left to find a friend of mine who had arranged to make the voyage with me. She knew the ship quite well from her many passages back and forth. She also knew many of the ship's workers and police in the city. I told her that I was concerned that the storage room might not be safe for storing our belongings because of thieves. She followed me into the room and yanked the tarp off the rice sacks, revealing a Vietnamese man a few years older than me. Being the savvy girl that she was, she knew Vietnamese from her trading. She asked him in Vietnamese what he was doing there. He told her to put the tarp back over his head so that he would not be discovered. We learned that he was a Vietnamese soldier who had made off from his squadron in the hopes of returning to his family that he desperately missed. He had been away for a long time. He pleaded with us to keep his discovery a secret, and he promised not to take any of our belongings. We covered him back up, and later, we went back to check on him. After the ship was far out in the lake, we encouraged him to sit with us on the deck. We decided to try to help him, so we invited him to eat lunch and dinner with us. It seemed that he would be safer blending in with us instead of trying to hide in the storage room, where someone else might accidentally fall upon him. While eating, we offered him advice on how to leave the ship once it docked in Phnom Penh. We told him that if he left the ship gradually, with everyone else, it would be less likely that he would be stopped to have his papers checked. If he waited until almost everyone had disembarked, or if he was one of the first people off the ship, his chances of getting away without being checked would be greatly reduced. After arriving in Phnom Penh, we saw that he was able to leave successfully, and we watched him walk away into the busy crowds. Once in the big city, it would be easier for him to go eastward to Vietnam. In retrospect, I feel that this incident of helping him had positive karmic consequences for me years later, when I found myself in a similar situation trying to escape a difficult and very different place.

Everyone who traveled around Cambodia needed papers that were very specific as to where a person was traveling to and from. It was supposed to be a deterrent to screen out Khmer rebels who traveled around the country, not that it was effective. If a person was stopped without them carrying the proper papers and the explanation seemed strange, a person could be thrown in jail for a couple of days, and all the money they carried could be confiscated. As I frequently went from place to place, I paid to have papers made up in Phnom Penh. With money, a person could buy just about anything there. My friends did the same—the papers looked authentic enough. If I wanted to travel between cities in Cambodia, I would normally have to go to the local government office to apply for the papers and stamp, and even these did not look official enough. This was troublesome and time consuming. It was one of the many new and different ways that the new Vietnamese-controlled government would collect money other than through customs. My friends and I did not believe that each person should have to be monitored while traveling from region to region, within our native country. After I had been working in the trade for about a year, I began to carry a great deal of money with me, to make trading easier. As my friends and I often carried around US$1,500 to US$2,000 in gold hidden in our money pouches in our pants, we could not afford to have our earnings confiscated. The police, for the most part, I had learned from my brother, did not care to check papers unless there was a reason to believe that a person was up to something. In this case, for our protection, we always had the appropriate papers with us when we traveled. I was stopped two times, but the papers that I had looked authentic enough. There was a lot of corruption within some levels of the government and among some of the police, so it was important to gain street smarts to avoid problems.

Another indication of the Khmer Rouge soldiers' ignorance was that they never learned how to take advantage of these businesses in the cities. Not only did they stand out like a rotting branch on a tree, but they often did not carry any paperwork at all with them, which often landed them in jail.

Travel by train was another way that I was able to go around Cambodia. At that time, there were two trains that left each day from Battambang, the largest city near Sisophon: the local and the express trains. From 9:00 a.m. every day, the local train bound for Phnom Penh left. I usually took the local train with my friends instead of the express because we could go first class cheaper than second class on the express. The first class had beds to nap on, and we usually enjoyed the longer trips, as we could spend the entire day sharing jokes and laughing. As I was so young, I was very popular to have along on those group business tours. My young age made me very unique and seem particularly bold, which earned me respect from my much older trading partners. If we took the local train, we would reach the end of the line in Pursat city at around 3:40 p.m. We rarely stayed in hotels anywhere in Cambodia, but instead, stayed at a network of friends' homes throughout the country. We stayed with a friend's family, in an extra room in Pursat, near the train station. We stored all of our merchandise there too. We would leave from Pursat on the local train for Phnom Penh the next day around 8:00 a.m. On this journey, the train traveled near Kampong Chhnang, where it stopped for lunch. In the evening, we would arrive at Phnom Penh's Central Station.

The view leaving Kampong Chhnang was breathtaking. From the window, a lush tropical forest could be seen. Coconut, mango, and banana trees were thick everywhere. Bamboo grew tall, and thick, in dense clusters.

Occasionally, teak and other hardwood trees could be seen. There was lush hilly green everywhere. Dense, unpopulated forests covered small hills and knolls. There was also the intermittent monkey that could be seen in the trees. It was a beautiful ride, along the way to Phnom Penh. All kinds of wild flowers added hints of color to the very deep green that was everywhere.

I enjoyed using the trains the best. They were the cleanest and smoothest way to travel. The train moved along smoothly over the tracks, despite the occasional tinkle of glassware and the occasional clank of the train cars. I enjoyed having the larger windows to see the countryside, as well as greater room to stretch out in. It was by steam engine locomotive that the trains powered their way around the countryside. In all of Cambodia, the entire fleet of contemporary trains that did not require wood consisted of four trains. They were usually reserved for the express travel between the provinces and the capital city.

Another combination of cities that we traded between was Koh Kong, Phnom Penh, and Svay Rieng. Koh Kong is in the south, on the Gulf of Thailand. Some of the goods in that market were brought by boat from the markets in Ko Samui, an island in southern Thailand. Svay Rieng is near the Vietnamese–Cambodian border, in the southeast. I could get the same merchandise in Koh Kong that I could in Sisophon for about the same price, without traveling clear across the country. My friends and I would travel by express bus on this route over Highway 4, the largest highway built in Cambodia at that time. As our bus could travel at 100–120 kilometers per hour, we could usually make the trip down to Koh Kong from Phnom Penh in about three to four hours. We would always stay in downtown Koh Kong with people who we bought a lot of merchandise from. The beautiful, white-yellow sand beaches of Koh Kong made it a favorite city of mine. The deep blue green hue of the ocean was quite clear for many meters out. The city was built on the slope of a tall mountain that quickly sloped down onto the beach. Coconut palms grew right out over the beach and sometimes over the water. My friends and I would often go swimming there when we visited the city. Life was very pleasant for us on these visits, despite the skirmishes of Khmer rebels that often went on, not far away, in the nearby jungle. As we could stay with people who we bought things from, a stay there was very affordable. After spending time in Koh Kong, my friends and I would make the trip back to Phnom Penh, then take the bus over Highway 1 toward the Vietnamese border to the city of Svay Rieng. I could sometimes sell items there for even greater profit than in Phnom Penh. There was very little that I would buy there, as the Vietnamese products and other products from around Cambodia were already very marked up in price in that market.

All across Cambodia, sellers who were very happy about our business would open up their homes to us. In Cambodia, it was the custom, excluding the capital city, where thieves and robbers were becoming more and more common. A person had to be wary of pick-pockets. I feel that the main reason why I was never robbed was that I appeared to be too young to have had any money worth bothering for. In fact, I never saw anyone my age doing my business. I had one friend who had almost US$2,000 in gold stolen. It happened so strangely that it may have been that his money pouch fell out of his pants, instead. The money pouch was nowhere to be found in the area where he thought he may have dropped it. The accident decimated his business profits for that year. I usually kept my savings, except for my working money, in Sisophon with my elder sister, Paht. Other boys of my age did not venture from home very often. And many people stayed stagnant in the poverty that was still very common throughout the countryside. I was leading a very different kind of life and feeling very lucky. Although I was only fifteen, it was remarkable that I had over US$2,000 in gold safely tucked away with my elder sister, Paht. My family was prospering.

In my family, uncles and aunts were all very proud of me, except for one uncle. This uncle already had a good amount of money from his trading business in Sisophon before I ever got started. Despite the poverty that my family had suffered, my uncle did not admit to having any money to help us. And when I began to do well with my business, and my family began to prosper as a result, he became jealous. He said bad things to us and tried to cause trouble among my family relations. He was always discouraging me, trying to get my father to stop me from traveling around, and saying, "I would lose all my money, and more." He did not know what he was talking about, as he had no idea of the money that I kept with my sister and of the money that I carried with me for my business use. He said I would lose my family's money, and then no one in my family would have anything to eat. To my own amazement, it was not long before I began making more than my uncle in Sisophon. Actually, I began to make in one day what it would take him two months to make. Eventually, my immediate family decided to stay away from him, just ignoring his petty admonitions, instead of allowing a bigger family dispute to develop. My father was always very lenient in letting me try whatever I wanted to do. He knew from the past, that there was no changing my mind, once an idea entered my head.

I was more than able to pay back to my brother the money that I used to start my business. In addition, I gave him US$300 in gold, enough to cover the cost of his wedding. I was doing well, and this was exciting for me, as the money and success was allowing me to have an additional sense of freedom that was not allowed in the Khmer Rouge village. As I was able to travel cheaply with friends and not have to pay for accommodations, around the country, I was able to eliminate many expenses, allowing me to save more. I always tried to buy those items that people seemed to like the most. I always sold everything, and only rarely did I ever have to sell at a loss. I was a hard negotiator, and I learned well the different tricks of the trade. I often sold to wholesalers in Phnom Penh, selling by the dozen instead of individually. This made for the quicker movement of my wares and allowed me to have more time to play with friends in the city.

I was able to travel to many places throughout the country. However, I never visited Angkor Wat, Cambodia's most famous temple. It was never really on the way, and it was not very safe, as the Khmer rebels made it a very unfortunate place for visitors by planting landmines everywhere. My mother had taken me to Angkor when I was a baby. One of my favorite pictures, destroyed in the village, was one of my mother holding me up, when I was a baby, while standing in front of the ancient temple. It had been framed, and it hung on the wall of our house before the Khmer Rouge takeover in 1975.

After returning from one of my trips to Phnom Penh, I learned that Lem had died. She died an early death just as my mother had. At the age of forty-eight, she died of some peculiar disease that I think today might have been diagnosed as tuberculosis. For about a month, she lost a great deal of weight. In the days before her passing, she began to cough up blood. Her death was very sad for me, as her strong spirit bolstered my own during those rough years of village life. She helped us survive, and she was always filled with so much love for us. She was a good woman, as was my biological mother. It was very sad news to hear about Lem's death. We all loved her and missed her terribly. I respect her memory as much as I do my own mother's.

In the same year, a famous museum, Tuol Sleng, opened up in Phnom Penh. It is most widely known for the map of Cambodia formed by placing skulls side-by-side to shape out the borders and interior of the country—a memorial to the Cambodian holocaust. At the site of the museum, a death camp once existed where thousands of Cambodians who had lived in the capital city perished. Most of them were educated people, or people who showed resistance for one reason or another to Pol Pot's takeover. Ominous exhibits were displayed. The original site was that of an old school. After the soldiers had converted the school into a death camp, rooms were used for various kinds of torturous killings. One exhibit showed how they drowned some of their victims by tying ropes around their feet. Their arms and legs would be bound. They would slowly be lowered into a pool of water. When their stomach muscles finally gave out, they drowned in the water. A large sugarcane field grew at the site. All around the field, the bodies of those who were killed during their slaughters were used as fertilizer to keep the sugarcane nourished. A very sick-minded group of people masterminded the many kinds of torture practiced there. Barbed wire prevented prisoners from jumping off of balconies and out of windows so they could not commit suicide to escape the tortures they were enduring. It was an awful place but an important reminder of the potential for evil that exists within humanity.

It was amazing to me that the Cambodian government still could not stop the rebel skirmishes in the countryside. The only sensible explanation for the Khmer Rouge's continued existence seemed to be the instability of the new Cambodian puppet government and the sick, ignorant, and emotionally laden mission of the Khmer Rouge soldiers that spurred them into continued fighting.

My two best friends in Phnom Penh, after working alongside me for a couple of years, ended their business. I missed not being around them in the market, but I was still more than welcome in their homes. The Khmer Rouge were again causing problems with the buses, trains, and cars throughout the country. They would shoot at buses during the day, and every now and then, an unfortunate bus or train would ride over landmines that were planted at night. Many were killed during these incidents. Transportation around Cambodia was getting more dangerous. I continued on, despite this, because the money I was earning for my family was helping them tremendously. Somehow I felt safe enough.

I made a new friend, Lim, who was another widow at age twenty-eight. We began to team up, working alongside each other in the market. I sometimes stayed with her during my week-long visits to Phnom Penh. She had a bad premonition about the growing tide of Khmer Rouge skirmishes throughout the country. It was just like in the early 1970s before they seized control. Some of her family had already left and made it all the way to America. She was beginning to feel that she should do the same. It was through her that I began to consider such a fantastical idea of moving to such a faraway place, away from the wars that I had known all of my life. We worked alongside each other for almost a year. I was very sad to see her go, when one day I learned that Lim had left Phnom Penh for the big refugee camp in Thailand in hopes of getting passage to America. She was fearful of the Khmer Rouge rising to power again. The instability of the Vietnamese-sponsored government made for a very uncertain future, especially with the many different factions all vying for power.

Another friend that I had met about the same time as Lim was Malradi. He and I would spend a great deal of time traveling around Cambodia together. Malradi, Succun, and I would also go to famous places around Phnom Penh. Together we saw the Royal Ballet perform traditional Cambodian dancing at the Performing Arts Pavilion, a large attractive outdoor theater at the Royal Palace, in the center of Phnom Penh. Many people from the countryside never traveled to Phnom Penh, so they were unable to see the famous Cambodian Royal Ballet perform the epic poem, the *Reamker*—the Cambodian tradition of the *Ramayana*—in the theater. This famous story, so embedded in Cambodia's ancient history, was taught to me when I was a child, by viewing shadow puppet shows in Sisophon. The shadow puppet shows were no longer as popular as they were before the Khmer Rouge had taken control, but maybe someday they would revive. The music, the famous *Pinpeat* Ensemble, was familiar to everyone, as it could be heard everywhere throughout Cambodia during festivals and even sometimes in the markets. The music of the *Ramayana* is most uniquely remembered by the sounds of the bamboo xylophone. Art and dance were slowly reviving after being obliterated by Pol Pot's communists. It was beautiful to see the traditional Cambodian dancing by the Royal Ballet, and especially to see the brilliant and ostentatious costumes of the performance. I loved watching the dancers move their head from side to side and contort their bodies to the intricate movements of the dance. There were still a few dancers left who had somehow managed to survive the years of the Khmer Rouge holocaust.

It was on the trips that I made around Cambodia with Malradi, trading, that I learned about the big camp in Thailand called Khao I Dang, where Cambodians were able to get passage to America, France, Australia, or New Zealand, through the United Nations. I became interested in the possibility of going to America or France, places far away from the turmoils of my home country. For the time being, the country seemed to have improved, but who was to say that the weak Vietnamese government would not be toppled by the strengthening Khmer Rouge guerillas. But then again, the Vietnamese were never very popular with the Cambodian people from their contentious historical relations.

The political situation seemed to be getting worse. I would not let myself endure, once again, the horrors of another war. In Phnom Penh, on the Cambodian public radio broadcast from New York City, I learned, after several months of listening, that the situation had stabilized along the border, where hundreds of thousands of refugees from Cambodia had fled during the past four years. The largest refugee camp, the Khao I Dang holding facility, was the only one that could truly help people attain sponsorships to other countries. From listening to the discussions, I was able to confirm stories that I had heard about refugees being turned back by the Thai government until just recently. I was surprised that other people in the world knew about our plight and that the United Nations, a powerful group of nations that I was just learning about, was actually working very hard to try to alleviate the problems in my country. Along with the positive reports of Khao I Dang, there were also the dismal reports from other holding facilities along the border. Many of the other refugee camps housed thousands of former Khmer Rouge soldiers, who continued their crimes within the barbed wire fences of the refugee camps, torturing the common people who unwittingly arrived there. The Khao I Dang camp was the only one that seemed safe.

In Phnom Penh, one of my friends, Keng, tried to dissuade me from attempting to cross the border. Shortly after the Vietnamese takeover, Keng and his father had attempted to make the crossing into Thailand together. While waiting on the Thai side of the border, he and hundreds of others were hoarded together on buses. Supposedly they were going to be taken to a holding facility there, so they entrusted themselves to the Thai soldiers driving the bus. The bus stopped near the border area, near a tall mountain, and the soldiers told them that they must go down the mountain, and at the lower end, Vietnamese soldiers would be waiting for them, to take them back to Cambodia. People were dismayed when they realized what was happening and that they would not be granted asylum in Thailand. The Thai government was not happy having hundreds of thousands of refugees entering their country, and the government did not feel it was their problem to remedy the situation. The Thai soldiers were ordered to send the refugees back.

Keng followed the instructions of the Thai soldiers, following the pathway down the hill, near the temple of Preah Vihear, on the northern border of Cambodia. Busloads of people were unloaded, and people walked down the increasingly steep trails. Suddenly the Thai soldiers began shooting, to encourage them to not linger long near the top. People began moving down the hill quickly. Some people lost their footing and stumbled. In some parts of the mountain, the pathway became so steep that people had to hang onto trees and bushes to help themselves down. Some people fell almost one hundred meters to their deaths. Then explosions were suddenly heard as people stepped on unseen landmines that covered the area. It was a trick, by the Thai soldiers, to eliminate many of the refugees in this way. People who were injured were moaning everywhere. If a person did not follow the people directly in front, then they ran the risk of stepping on a landmine. Keng's father was not so fortunate, meeting his death suddenly, after stepping on a landmine. He and Keng had survived so much together, in the Khmer Rouge village. It seemed like such a waste for his father to die on the mountain, in such a cruel way. Keng told me this story to discourage me from going to Thailand. He would never attempt to leave Cambodia again.

After listening to the public radio for months, I felt that the situation had changed along the border, and I knew of others who had also decided to try to make the crossing to Thailand. My friend Malradi and I discussed the idea of trying it together. If fighting started again, our trading would have to end, and, perhaps, we again would be faced with another revolution. The new government seemed unable to remedy the Khmer Rouge threat, and much of the country's roads and public buildings were still in shambles. Our brief period of freedom would come to an end, if the situation did not change. Our enjoyable life would disintegrate, washing away like sand on the beach.

I discussed my idea of going to America with my father. He did not say anything to try to discourage me, but he did seem a little upset. He really did not want the family to be separated again. He agreed that I might find better opportunities in another country, especially in America or France, if I were able to get sponsored to live there, but he really did not want me to leave. I could tell. There were also the dangers of crossing over to Thailand, even in that time of relative stability on the border. My father also knew well that he would be unable to dissuade me from going, if I chose to do so. I was not exactly naïve about the challenges I might face, but I was full of ambition for a better life. My father told me that he did not know how to help me, and he told me not to tell others about my plans.

In a couple of weeks, I made plans, as everyone thought, to go to Phnom Penh. However, the secret was that after leaving to go toward Phnom Penh, I would immediately return, to stay at a hotel in Sisophon. I would then go with a guided group over the Thai border. My mind was made up. Gah (now knick-named Lye Lye) brought my clothes to the hotel. She cried, asking me to bring her with me, but I did not want to involve her in my plan. She was still so small. I did not want to lose her in the jungle or see her get hurt. I was certainly going to miss my little sister. I was not sure that I would make it myself. My father sensed that I might try to go across the border to Thailand, and he sent his goodbye wishes through her. He did not meet me at the hotel for fear of others learning that I was attempting to leave. He did not want any unforeseen problems coming about later, as a result, for me or my brother and sisters. I said a sad goodbye to my sister at 7:00 a.m. She was thirteen, and I was sixteen years old.

8

JOURNEY THROUGH THE JUNGLE

Malradi and I decided to cross the border together with a guide that we were introduced to, through his sister, in Phnom Penh. The cost for each of us would be US$400. It was the only way to go across, as it was too dangerous, and it was unlikely to get over to Thailand without a guide. There were too many challenges, with landmines and soldiers of various factions that we might encounter, along the trails. Later that morning, a group of about twelve of us left Sisophon and walked west with our guide. I had never met anyone else in the group. They were a wide assortment of men and women who were determined to make the crossover to Thailand in search of a better life. We walked to a village called Maka and stayed there until dark. Maka was only a two-hour walk from Sisophon, but the guide did not dare take us close to the border during daylight because the Thai border patrol and Khmer rebels in the jungle were dangerous. We stayed at his partner's house in Maka for a day. Around 9:00 p.m., we left Maka, continuing westward through a large rice field, which took us about an hour to cross. We then walked through the dense jungle. Everything was very quiet, except for the nighttime bird calls of the jungle and the sounds of insects chirping. There were lots of bamboo and large trees everywhere. We were very aware of the landmines everywhere as well, which the guide helped us to bypass. At about 2:00 a.m., we rested for about two hours in the middle of the jungle. We each brought our own bottle of water and a little food. At about 4:00 a.m., we continued onto the Cambodian Camp of Sihanouk Soldiers, also known as Chumrun Tamai.

It was quite dark, and you could still see their faces, but suddenly out of the jungle, a group of thugs, or possibly former Khmer Rouge soldiers, appeared. Every one of them had a gun. They were wearing the clothes of the Khmer Rouge, all dressed in black or green. Our hearts stopped. We thought, *This is it.* They told us to stand away from each other. They searched us one by one. They were looking for gold or money that we had brought. Each person gave up their gold or Thai baht. They told me to step aside, while having everyone else line up next to each other. They said I was too dark, that I would not have any money. "Don't waste your time with him," the leader of the group of thugs said. I stood aside. They searched all the others' clothes, under their shirts, underwear, socks, and shoes. They made them take their clothes off. I was panicking. All of them had guns, at least ten robbers. Some even had hand grenades on their belts. Then after the search, they all took their money and everything they had. Our guide did not bring very much with him, but he had to give up all he had as well. Then they suddenly left. My small blue packet of gold in my shoe was still there, and in place. They did not take it. I still have the small miniature blue bag that carried my gold to this day. I was the only one who was left with money, and it was more than enough to be used for our group. But I did not tell them that I still had my gold. Only Malradi knew, my best friend. I could not trust anyone.

We were lucky that they left us in the jungle. Everyone redressed, and we continued on our plan to get to the border. Our next stop was Chumrun Tamai. At this camp, the Chumrun Tamai soldiers, whom our guide knew, were a faction that was in support of a free Cambodia, an anti-Khmer Rouge and anti-Vietnamese group. This group of soldiers did not care if we left Cambodia or not. It was the Thai soldiers, the Vietnamese soldiers, the Heng Samrin Cambodian soldiers, and the Khmer Rouge that we had to be concerned about. The coalitions were changing frequently. But for the time being, we had a place to relax in the Chumrun Tamai camp. In fact, we were able to clean up and rest there for two days before going on to Thailand. In the camp, our guide introduced us to another guide who would take us onto the camp in Thailand.

We left Chumrun Tamai at about 6:00 p.m. at night, with our new guide. Both our guides were Cambodian. I did not know how they knew the areas so well. We walked carefully through the dense jungle. We would walk for a short while, then stop, then walk again. We did not want to be met up with another group of robbers again, so carefully and as quietly as possible, we walked on through the jungle. We continued in this way until about 4:00 a.m., right before sunrise so no one could see us easily. We did not meet up with any soldiers or gunfire as we crossed through the dense foliage. We walked in water that was up to our necks, and then walked in water that reached only our knees or ankles. The guide finally announced that we had made it into Thailand, and that soon we would be approaching the Khao I Dang refugee camp, the largest holding facility of Cambodian refugees within the Thai border. Around 4:00 a.m., the soldiers were not heavily staffed around the camp. Fences with sharp barbed wire prevented people from either climbing in or out of the camp.

Every one hundred meters, there was a guard station, some on the ground, others five meters off the ground. Many Cambodians met their death trying to cross into the camp, as the Thai soldiers did shoot if they saw any movement along the fence. We stayed back in the jungle, while our guide crossed a narrow rice field to approach a guard who was standing on the side of the fence. Each of us was worth 1,000 Thai baht, about US$5 at the time of business, to the Thai soldier. If a mistake was made, or if the soldier decided to renege, our guide would be shot, and the rest of us would be chased back into the jungle, with a slim-to-none chance of successfully crossing the border back into Cambodia. Our guide motioned us to come to where he stood, and we all furtively made our way through a hidden opening under the fence.

The guide continued on with us into the refugee camp, to the house where his family lived. My good friend Malradi and I did not know anyone in the camp, so we were allowed to stay hidden with his family for two days. We had to be cautious, as we did not have the registry tags to wear to show that we were in the camp legally. We spent a couple of days cleaning up, adjusting to the camp, and getting our bearings. My friend and I soon found a friendly old couple who would let us stay with them in their hut. They did not really want us to stay with them because Malradi and I were there illegally, but they were sympathetic to us, and they decided to help. Non-registered refugees who were discovered by Thai soldiers in the camp were beaten along with those who hid them. The non-registered refugees were sent back to Cambodia. We had no desire to be sent back, or to be beaten, for that matter, so we had to minimize all time outside of the hut.

It was very sad to leave behind my family and many friends in Cambodia. The realization became clear as the weeks turned into months that I may have made a terrible mistake, choosing an illusory dream to go to the camp. I really began to wonder what I had done with my life. I often wondered about my friends in different parts of Cambodia who were somewhere trading, probably wondering about me a little too, thinking, "Where did the little merchant go?" Apart from Malradi, my two best friends, Succun and Ain, who were still in Phnom Penh, probably figured out what I had done. I had talked with them a little about my idea of going to America, and they would most likely let others who were close to me know as well. I knew that I could still return at any time, although it would be just as dangerous as before to make the crossing back over the border again. I would also have to pay the guide again to take me back, but I waited, hanging on for some opportunity ahead.

9

HIDING OUT

In the first year in the camp, I started out with about US$1,200 in gold, which I kept with me in a small blue pouch inside my pants. Luckily the thieves in the jungle never found it. My luck in being the "black boy," being so dark and young compared to other Cambodians, was the reason that the robbers were so sure I couldn't have anything of value on me. All of what was in the blue pouch was all of what I had saved up from my trading business around Cambodia. I always kept it with me, and every night, I would dig a hole in the ground, in the floor of my hut, to bury the money. I thought of my stepmother, Lem, who had buried the family pictures each night in the village. I was careful not to put the pouch in any place where it might get wet, or get lost, like burying it outside the hut where others could dig it up. I always had to be wary of thieves and the possibility of being robbed—it happened often in the camp. After living in the camp for about a year, my money supply dwindled to only about US$250. It was the point of no return. I had to either go back or stay. If I dwindled my gold down anymore, which I would with the necessary cost of eating, I would be unable to pay the guide to take me back. If my money supply did run out, and I still was unable to get a registration card, I would have to turn myself in, or I would starve. In that case, I would run the risk of being beaten severely by the Thai soldiers, before being sent back into the jungle on the Cambodian side of the border. Malradi and I decided to stick it out.

Some refugees in the camp had relatives in other countries. Relatives would sometimes send them money. If a person was of legal status, life would be much easier in the camp. The only way that I could send mail back to Cambodia was through a guide, which I did, as soon as I could after entering the camp, to let them know that I was safe. My family did not know if I had made it across, until they received my letter. I was so thankful that I was able to let my family know that I was alive, yet I was not really able to know for sure, if the guide made it successfully back or not. My chances of running into the same guide again were slim. That letter cost me about US$200 to be delivered. All I had was his word that it would be delivered, so a person had to go with their gut feeling about the integrity of a guide before handing over the money. In Cambodia, mail was still not a possibility, because letters would be opened up, and anything of interest or value, would be taken. From the camp, even if I were living there legally, there was no way to communicate back home, except through a guide, as the Thai and Cambodian governments did not have an agreement for the mail between the two countries. As my money supply dwindled, I knew I would not be able to send them another letter, if I decided to stay. I would not be able to make enough money, even if I were to somehow get legalized in the camp, to raise the money needed to return home with a guide to see from my family. I had left about US$2,000 with my elder sister, Paht, but there was no way for her to send any of the money to me in the camp from Cambodia. At least I had left a small personal legacy behind for my family, if they were to never hear from me again.

Other refugees in the camp, both legal and illegal, carried money with them, as I did. I knew well what starvation was like from the village life, yet I was able to still buy reasonable amounts of food to get by. There were many ways to make money in the camp, to buy extra food, or other supplies, when a person had a legal registration number, but unfortunately being in the camp illegally, I did not have one. As a result, Malradi and I could not work.

We also had to be especially wary of the low-life, that considered stealing as an appropriate means of getting what they needed. If Malradi and I were robbed, with no money to buy food, we would wind up totally at the mercy of the Thai soldiers. My friend, Malradi, and I stayed in the same hut. There was nothing to do, except to sit, eat, and sleep. We could not risk walking around the camp freely while still remaining there illegally.

After about one year of living this way in the camp, the Thai police decided to do a thorough search for people illegally hiding in the camp. The number of us had grown substantially over the year. Malradi and I had to resort to digging a hole in the kitchen floor of the hut, to hide from the searching Thai soldiers. We made a narrow opening to the hole, just wide enough to squeeze through, and then several feet underground, we dug out a small chamber, small enough for both of us to fit inside together. Not a lot of dirt was removed, just enough. We spread the excess dirt around the dirt floor of the hut's kitchen area. Bamboo wood, that was used for making fires for cooking, was piled over the opening. The weak ground was also covered with other lightweight objects in the kitchen area. Over the area, the older couple hung underwear, and other laundry items. Everything was made to look normal. The Thai soldiers did not like going near the underwear that was hanging to dry. It was taboo. From down below, we could hear the Thai soldiers walking above when they searched our hut. We could also hear them talking but could not make out what they said. Neither of us understood Thai very well. We were happy though, when we thought that they said that the hut was clear. *We made it,* we thought to ourselves. During the search, we stayed underground from 5:00 a.m. until 4:00 p.m. in the afternoon. The older couple above asked us frequently during the day if we needed any water, and if we were all right. As we did not know whether the soldiers would return, we waited until the older couple told us when it was safe to come up. It was very quiet in the ground below the hut, as everyone in the camp was silent, for fear of themselves or people hiding with them of being caught and sent back to the border. The air was difficult to breathe, and when we finally got out, we were very sick and nauseous. That night, we could still go to the UN infirmary, operated by the Red Cross to see nurses and get medicine. We were always safe in the infirmary, as the Thai soldiers did not want to be seen roughing up the refugees. The Red Cross workers could not do anything about our illegal status, but they were more than willing to help us with medicine.

We were very relieved to have made it through their search, but we both had huge doubts as to whether or not we could continue on in this way. On the day after the search, on a Saturday morning, as I remember, a large convoy of buses came into the camp. On the large microphones that were spread around the camp, announcements could be heard that anyone wishing to emigrate to Malaysia could take an interview test with the Malaysian Embassy and sponsorships could be arranged. My friend and I both wanted out of the camp terribly. It seemed like an endless situation for us. I did not want to go to Malaysia, but my friend did not care, so we immediately went to the building, where he could register with the Malaysian Embassy. As we were among some of the first there, he was able to take the test immediately and was matched with a sponsor. After hearing this, I approached Malradi's sponsor too. His sponsor told me that he could not sponsor anyone else, and that he already had too many to sponsor. I offered him 4,000 Thai baht, about US$150, most of the money that I had left, to sponsor me, but he refused. By that time, there were already crowds around us, and all of the sponsorships were filled. My friend got on one of the buses and sat near the window. I was in disbelief to be separated from my good friend after so long and after sharing so many challenges together, crossing the border, and hiding out with him for the past year in the camp. A sudden sense of loneliness and fear overwhelmed me. I did not know what would happen to me. Maybe our survival together was only meant for him. As the bus pulled away, we watched each other, waving goodbye. Grief and despair overcame me, as I began to weep.

I quickly got back to my hut, so I would not be caught by a Thai soldier. I was still an illegal in the camp. I felt that I made a terrible mistake of ever coming to Thailand. I could not sleep that night. The anguish of being left alone was too much. I could not write letters to my family, as I could not afford to pay for their delivery. My family did not know that I was safe, but then I did not know either.

I stayed up all night, grief-stricken, not sure how I could continue to keep hiding in the camp. I wanted to see my family again, but I could not easily return. I was glad for my friend, but I was also angry about the unfairness of everything in my life.

10

KHAO I DANG REFUGEE CAMP

At about 4:00 a.m., I was surprised by announcements on the microphones. It was Sunday morning. I did not sleep at all during the night, so I was already awake to hear the public address. The announcement, in Cambodian, went something like this: "UNHCR (United Nations High Commissioner for Refugees) and the Thai government have agreed to grant registration cards to anyone living illegally in the camp. A new building has been constructed, to expedite the issuance of new papers and registration numbers, for those living without the proper identification in the camp. People must report immediately to this building to receive their papers." I was in shock, as I could not believe that it was true. It seemed like a ruse. I walked over to the area, and I was surprised to find a totally new building that had been constructed. It was a small, simple building that had been built overnight. I did not even know that it had been built. All around the building was a barbed wire fence, and there were many Thai soldiers guarding the building. There were also many Americans and other UN personnel around, loading large boxes and camera equipment into the building. The Thai soldiers surely would not hassle me with the UN people all around. I decided to risk it. I felt at that point that I also had nothing to lose anymore. I was one of the first to approach the building.

We were told to form four lines. I was the fourth to get my picture taken and my new registration number. I could not believe the turn of events from the day before. I would no longer have to hide out illegally in the camp. I had tears of joy when I saw my new registration card. I felt jubilant, and there was hope that I would soon be able to get sponsorship to one of the more popular countries—like America, Canada, or Australia. I had so much appreciation for the UN workers that were there in the camp to help us. That was the first day in almost a year that I could walk around freely, without fear of being arrested.

Time continued to pass by in the camp. It was much easier for me, as I did not worry about being sent back to Cambodia, or being beaten up by the Thai soldiers. I was also then able to get UNICEF handouts of rice each week, being a legal alien in the camp. This was crucial in allowing me to survive, as my gold supply was to soon run out. I received more from UNICEF than I had ever received from the Khmer Rouge back in the village. Also, I was able to gain back my strength a little, being free to walk around the camp after having had to stay indoors for so long. One day, I ran across my friend, Lim, who I worked alongside in the markets of Phnom Penh. This was a wonderful chance happening. With so many people in the camp, I could have wandered around for ten years before coincidentally running into her. I had been living in the camp for about a year and a half, and she, for two years, by that time. I was so happy to find someone that I knew. I also was surprised to find a few other acquaintances there, that I had either done business with, or had met on trading trips around Cambodia. Lim said to me, "You are here too?" in surprise after recognizing me.

One day, I happened to have the chance to be near the truck driver who drove the daily water supply into the camp. I told him that if he could bring things into the camp, like cigarettes, or other products, I would buy them from him and then sell them in the camp. I did this spontaneously, without even thinking about it, so I was fortunate that the Thai man took to my idea instead of running me into the Thai soldiers. I had to find some way to keep from running out of all of my money. He and I developed a business relationship that lasted for the rest of the time that I remained in the camp. At first, he brought in small amounts of merchandise to sell to me, and then brought in much bigger amounts later. Inside the water jugs, he brought in an amazing assortment of goods all wrapped up. The Thai soldiers always checked the truck for refugees sneaking in and out, but they never looked inside the water jugs for merchandise. On a given day, he would sometimes come to the camp two or three times, so I would meet him during one of the times, to buy whatever he brought with him. I would keep the merchandise in my hut, and then go around to others in the camp, to see if they needed anything. I also sold items to a couple of women, who in turn, also sold them to others for profit. This was good, in that it kept me less conspicuous in the camp, in the event that the Thai soldiers found out and caused me any trouble. I was never that worried about getting in trouble, as we were discreet, not selling too much, just a few items at a time.

Although the camp was very close to the Thai city of Aranyaprathet, we never met any Thai people in the camp, except for the soldiers, and of course, my acquaintance, the waterman. We avoided all eye contact with the Thai soldiers, as we did not want to draw any attention to ourselves. As soldiers do in refugee camps, they sometimes beat anyone they do not like. They could never do this in front of any UN officials because they would likely be shamed or reprimanded by their commander. The UN which managed several volunteer organizations in the camp offered so much toward our survival. They kept careful observation of the Thai soldiers, guarding the camp, to prevent any abuses from occurring. It was also UNICEF and the Red Cross, I believe, that kept the water supply continually coming into the camp. Every day, we had to get up at 4:00 a.m. to get our water supply for the day, which was eight gallons. This was to be used for drinking, washing clothes, bathing, and cooking in our huts. The temperature was very hot, around 100°F on some days, with almost 80 percent humidity. We would have to wash ourselves at least twice a day, because of the heat and humidity. UNICEF also provided bamboo for us to make a bed, so we would not have to sleep on the ground on the dirt floors of our huts. We did not have air conditioning or electric fans, but at least we had the shade of our huts. It was certainly much better than day-to-day life under the Khmer Rouge in their controlled villages.

The camp was located in the middle of a jungle. Aside from small rice fields, on all sides of the camp, nothing could be seen outside the barbed wire of the camp. For the approximately 28,000 people that resided in the camp, there was nothing really for us to do other than to sit and wait. Every morning when we got up, we would ask each other if anyone had heard any news about being able to get sponsorships to other countries. Many of the first people that arrived in the camp, before the camp had been divided into sections, were never tested for their personal histories, but were given immediate sponsorships, as the officials in the refugee camp did not realize that the situation had changed in Cambodia. Some of the criminal instigators in the Khmer Rouge were then escaping for their lives into Thailand, just the same as many of the villagers had been doing in the years prior to 1979. The UN had tried for so long to enlist the Thai government's help in the refugee crisis that when approval was given for refugee holding camps, the UN granted immediate asylum to any refugee they could in sponsoring countries that wanted to help. As people kept showing up in swarms, it was eventually decided to issue IDs to everyone living in the camps and to mandate personal interviews to develop case histories, as sponsorships could not be arranged for everyone immediately.

The camp was divided into two sections while I was there, the KD section, for the long-timers, and the RC section, for the newcomers. I was in the RC section, as I arrived after 1982. I never did understand what the acronyms stood for, only what they meant. Both areas of the camp were separated by barbed wire, until the last few months that I was there. Neither groups associated with each other. The people in the KD section were given preferential treatment, since they were there the longest. However, during my last year in the camp, the situation changed, as new policies were put into effect that were related to the personal histories of the people in the different sections of the camp. The KD group was primarily made up of people who entered the Khao I Dang camp around 1979 and 1980, during the time when the Khmer Rouge were being ousted from power. Among many of the people who fled during that time, some of the refugees were former leaders and soldiers from the Khmer Rouge–controlled villages. Certainly not all. Many of the people who left Cambodia, immediately after the Vietnamese takeover, left because they felt they finally had a chance to get away from the political turmoil brewing in the country, and many did not have anything, or anyone to leave behind.

The people in the RC group came later when militant factions were causing more problems again. There was growing concern of another revolution, which would have made it the third, in a little more than a decade. Most of the people in the RC section were not involved with the Khmer Rouge, but were people like me, who had worked in servitude in the villages under their control. Once I had the freedom to walk around the camp freely with my registry tag, I preferred being separated from the KD, as I did not want to have to associate, on a day-to-day basis, with some of the people who caused so much damage to my home country. However, not all KD people were bad.

At first, I could not understand why the KD refugees were given preferential treatment, because I could tell that some were former Khmer Rouge members. But later, I realized that the KD had preferential treatment not just because they had been there the longest, but it was for the fact that the very friendly service workers in the camp had no idea that some of them were actually Khmer Rouge criminal instigators, who were also seeking asylum. It was first come, first serve, yet most of the people who were affiliated with the Khmer Rouge were detained for many years, failing interview after interview, and most were never granted sponsorship. Some of the good liars did manage to get through. Many of them were liars. Most of the people, who I knew of personally to be Khmer Rouge, were never granted a sponsorship, and they were eventually sent back to Cambodia. The 1951 Convention of Refugees set up rules not to grant asylum to war criminals or people suspected of being criminals against humanity.

When Malradi and I originally entered the camp, we did not know that the guide had brought us in on the KD side, or that there were two sections for that matter. Our guide was a former Khmer Rouge soldier himself, as it turned out. His family that was living in the camp was also affiliated with the Khmer Rouge. Once we became accustomed to the surroundings, we realized that we were going to have to tread the water carefully to survive, as we could not afford to make any enemies there. The older couple who we lived with us for the first year were former Khmer Rouge as well. The older man even admitted this to me, but they decided to help us, for whatever reason. Just as we could spot them, they could spot us. In actuality, we became friends, the four of us. Both of them had been remarried because they both lost their spouses during the revolution, either from starvation or from sickness, although they had been affiliated with the Khmer Rouge. I did not question why they helped us. Maybe it was for a type of redemption for their past affiliations. Or maybe it was because they did not have children of their own. I did not know; thankfully, there were two less people who supported their previous cause. We were also grateful for their generosity, as without them, we would not have survived the first year there.

The Khmer Rouge supporters could usually be spotted either from their usual southern accent from the Takao area, where the group apparently originated from in Cambodia, or from their conversations. Former Khmer Rouge would often talk a great deal about living in the forest, where the common people would have no reason to stay after the war. They also played some of their Khmer Rouge revolutionary music, that no one unaffiliated with the group would play. For the most part, they were what oil was to water, with oil being the Khmer Rouge, and water being the common people. When I was finally granted my registry tag, and legal papers, I was sent to the RC section, on the far side of the camp. It was not until the last year of my stay in the camp that I was able to see the older couple again. Both of them discussed with me how they could not understand how the revolution had gotten so out of control, and how it did not seem possible that so many people died. I appreciated them immensely for their help during my first year in the camp.

The older woman would frequently buy our food for us, so that we would not have to risk being seen in the open, without our registry tags. Neither of them were granted sponsorships because of their past affiliations, and eventually, they were sent back to Cambodia, despite their years of perseverance. In the years since, I have wanted to get in contact with them again, yet there is no way for me to trace their whereabouts—lost in the world, so to speak.

In 1983, the Reagan Administration passed new legislation that helped to prioritize the refugees to speed up the sponsoring process, as the numbers of refugees in the camps reached an alarming level.[2] It took several years to finally take effect, as personal case histories had to be developed. Finally, in the last year of my stay at Khao I Dang, as consistent personal histories were made known, the United Nations changed its treatment toward the KD, giving preferential treatment to the RC. The case histories revealed that many of the remaining KD people were not acceptable for sponsorships in countries, because of their past affiliations with the Khmer Rouge. Once this policy changed, the refugees in the RC section were easily able to arrange interview for themselves at the different consulates. As a result of the interviews, the KD group grew larger in comparison to the RC group, as people in the KD group were refused the opportunity to leave. Conversely, the last year that I was there, the RC registrants dwindled down to a small number of people, as most of us were granted sponsorships to other countries. I felt a small amount of justice in that.

Both sections of the camp made up about two square kilometers in area. Many of the UN and Red Cross workers lived in the city of Aranyaprathet, which was located just south of the camp. I had seen Caucasians before in Phnom Penh, but they were mainly from Cuba, the Soviet Union, and East Germany. Back in Cambodia, in the marketplace, I never talked with them, because I did not understand their languages. It was in the camp that I had the chance to see Americans, Canadians, and New Zealanders for the first time. The Americans seemed funny and pleasant, often smiling—very different from the stern looks that I saw on the faces of the white foreign-

2 Shawcross, The Quality of Mercy, p.337.

ers in the markets of Phnom Penh. They had very different personalities. I was not scared of the Americans, although they were generally much larger than I was.

On the RC side of the camp, a community formed of sorts. Small enterprises were flourishing, selling things, doing odd jobs for UNICEF, and teaching languages, dance, or other crafts that kept people busy. People could sew or make garments for better food. Luckily, I had made acquaintance with the truck driver, because that small business was allowing me to pay for my food and some French and English lessons too. At first I studied French, thinking that my chances of going to France would be easier than America. Also as my ex-sister-in-law made it there, several years before, I would, at least know someone there, although I had no idea where she lived then.

There were former professors in the camp, trying to get sponsorships abroad as well. I would not take lessons consistently, just from time to time, when I could afford them. I would usually take lessons in four- or five-month spurts. In the camp, I first began to learn my ABCs from a former professor of a university in Phnom Penh, who was also trying to emigrate. From him, I also learned a few basic phrases such as "How are you?" "How much does it cost?" et cetera. He was my favorite teacher, before I was able to take English lessons, sponsored by the INS (American Immigration and Naturalization Service). The professor would have a class in his little hut, for about thirty people at a time. Everyone would squeeze inside and try to understand his teachings. He charged each person about US$3 per lesson, which lasted about an hour. He was definitely a smart man to make so much money in the camp at one time. It was a constant struggle between deciding to eat and to save for more lessons. I knew that I had to learn some amount of either English or French to ever be able to be awarded a sponsorship.

At the beginning of my last year in the camp, UNICEF offered free English courses. This made it a lot easier for me to study English. My English was still very bad, but I began to learn slowly, important phrases for communicating and key vocabulary words. It was there where I met Elizabeth from

Texas. I thought that Elizabeth, who was the supervisor for the ESL program, was one of the kindest and most wonderful people that I had ever met. I only talked to her briefly, but she was always very cheerful and happy, and she always remembered my name. My friend, Sukkar, who worked for her as a translator, introduced me to her, and that is how I was able to get to know her and how she was able to learn my name. Later, she got promoted to a new position at the American Consulate, in Aranyaprathet, so she stopped coming to the camp.

In the camp, we also had a little temple, complete with a Buddhist priest, who was also trying to get passage to America, or elsewhere. So occasionally I would go there to pray. It was actually quite nice to have a priest there too, as his devoutness reminded me of my father, back in Sisophon, and the small temple there reminded me of a small temple not far from my old home. I also thought that it was convenient for all of us to have a temple in the camp.

In reality, the camp was only fifty kilometers from the area where I grew up, where my family was still living. The camp was also about seventy kilometers from the area where I had spent four years of my life in the forced labor camps. I often wondered about my family, not so far away. At least, in the camp, I had the freedom to study, to pray at the temple, and to eat what I liked, whenever I chose. I also had hope that I might eventually go to a country, far away from all of the fighting that I had known since I was a boy.

11

SKIRMISHES ON THE FENCE

The mood in the camp began to take a dismal turn. For the previous two weeks, there had been fighting during the night, just outside of the camp. The Khmer Rouge were skirmishing with Thai soldiers that were guarding the camp. The rebels were actually trying to get into the camp, to rob the refugees, as many of the rebels did not have any money. They were also protesting the recent change in preference by the UN, of giving the RC group the first opportunity at interviews, instead of those in the KD group, where many of their comrades were awaiting sponsorship. Some of the refugees in both sections of the camp actually had a fair amount of money, usually in the form of gold, stored away in their hut, buried in the ground of their floor, or elsewhere. It was primarily among the RC group where most of the refugees had the most money, as many already had relatives sending them money from other countries. The rebels would sometimes make their way into the camp, killing some of the refugees, while robbing them. Aside from money, they also took clothes and other items. If an illegal refugee were robbed, this could spell doom for that person in the not-so-distant future, as they would be forced out of their hut to look for work in order to buy food. Once they were discovered by the Thai soldiers, their life would be precariously uncertain, as the person could be beaten and left on the Cambodian side of the jungle, with no means or understanding of how to return home.

One night, a couple of Thai soldiers were killed as a result of skirmishes near the fence. On the following day, there was growing apprehension about the possibility of a break-in. People tended to stay in their huts and avoided walking near the fence at all times. Also, for the fear of the Thai soldiers assuming that a Cambodian refugee was affiliated with the rebels, it was important to stay far away from the fence. To the Thai soldiers, all Cambodians were the same, and a nuisance, coming into their country and now coming over and shooting fellow Thai citizens as well. During these uprisings when there were reports of rebel soldiers getting into the camp, refugees in the camp would run in the opposite direction, creating a state of pandemonium.

That night, another group of illegal refugees, just as I had once been, came under the fence, but this time, they were spotted. Obviously, their guide was unaware of the heightened security on the fence, along with the problems in the previous days. All of the people in the group got away, except for one. The next day, early in the morning, we were told to get out of our hut to see "the murderer first hand, who had killed the Thai soldiers in the days before." The illegal refugee was charged with being a rebel, who had come into the camp to murder and steal. Announcements were made over the loud speakers that everyone had to watch the Cambodian man when he came by our hut, or else we would be punished. People cried in the camp as they watched what the Thai soldiers did to the man. They strung him up on a large cross, like the Christian Cross, tying his hands and feet tightly to the wood, displaying him around the camp on the back of a truck. I was horrified. All of us knew that it could be any one of us that could have been caught crossing over the border into the camp, and that he was truly very unlucky and unfortunate to be caught. The public address speakers proclaiming that he was the murderer added to the tension. We all knew that he would be executed later in the day, and that there was nothing that anyone could do to stop it. The poor man, a few years older than me, was sobbing and was obviously frightened. My heart went out to him, because I saw myself in him. I wondered when the suffering would ever end.

12

THE INTERVIEW

After five and a half years of living in the camp, my name was drawn, among several others, to go to an interview with the French government. My application was being considered for sponsorship with a Parisian family. The American government invited me for an interview shortly after that. I had no idea what my prospects were for either country. I was very hopeful for either, but mainly the latter. I felt it would be more realistic for me to go to France, as it seemed that more of the refugees from Cambodia seemed to be accepted there much more readily than to America. At the small library that was built in the camp, I began to look through books on America. I could not read the English writing very well at that time, but I was certainly able to understand from the pictures, that America must be a great country. One picture truly captured my imagination. It was a picture of the moon's landscape, with an American astronaut putting a flag in the ground. I could not believe it when I first saw the picture. The picture made me recall the power of the large American planes that flew overhead, when I was a child. I remember my sisters screaming from the immense vibration that one could feel, when they flew so close to my father's home. The Americans that I met, and observed in the camp, seemed so friendly, yet they must be very powerful people to be able to go to the moon. Not in a million years would Cambodia be able to put its flag up there. If I were to get sponsorship to go to America, it would be too good to be true.

For my interview with the Americans, I went with several others by bus to the consulate in Aranyaprathet a few kilometers away. At the consulate, there were three different desks for interviewing, and I was surprised that Elizabeth, the ESL supervisor whom I knew from Khao I Dang, was one of the interviewers. It was certainly my lucky day when my name was called by her. When she saw me, she recognized me. She was very kind to me during the interview, when she was going over my case history in detail. The questions that she asked me were similar to the following: "Where is your family?" "What were you doing in the years from 1975 to 1979?" It was her job to make sure that everything was correct on my application, before the information was sent to the INS. When the interview finished, she smiled and wished me the best of luck—at least, that is what I think she said, as my English was still pretty poor at that time.

In the following weeks, I did not hear from either the French or Americans yet, so I did not know how much longer it was going to take for me to get a sponsorship. I hoped that my years of perseverance would finally come to an end, and I hoped that I would not have to return to Cambodia, after going through so much. Honestly, I did not know where I would end up. I missed my family back in Sisophon, and I wondered about their safety with the growing Khmer Rouge presence in the area and increasing problems with landmines in the areas along the border and elsewhere. I heard that the area around Siem Reap and Angkor Wat had become increasingly dangerous, because of landmines that were planted every night by the Khmer Rouge guerrillas. Although Sisophon was also in the northwest area of Cambodia, I hoped that my hometown would be too large for them to try to terrorize with landmines or sniper fire. I wondered if my sister Met had married yet or how my Aunt Oiy and her family were doing. I had not heard from my friends around Cambodia from my trading business days, as it was nearly impossible to reach them by mail, even if I knew their addresses. I hoped that they remembered me. And I hoped that my father was still healthy and still able to work on the farm. Despite my trepidations of going so far away from my family and homeland, I felt deep inside that for my life, I was making the right decision. The camp life was manageable, but it was wearing on me, as I knew that in another few months, if I did not hear anything from the consulates, I would have to go back to Cambodia. I could not continue to wait indefinitely. If I were not chosen right away after my interviews, then it was likely that there was a problem, and that I would not be selected so easily in the future as well. It was a sad thought, but I felt optimistic. I was hopeful that Elizabeth would also come through for me; how lucky, I thought, to have her as my interviewer. There was karmic coincidence in that. She may have put a good word in for me, as I was a friend of her former interpreter, Sukkar. If Americans were all like her, America would be a wonderful country to live in, indeed! America, out of all the countries represented, had first choice to choose whom they would sponsor, so I was hopeful that I rated highly on my evaluation. If the Americans did not choose me, then hopefully the French government would.

It happened to me one day so quickly, and with so much surprise, that I could not believe it was really happening. On the big black board in the camp, and over the intercom in the camp, my name was selected. I had been chosen to go to the Chunbori camp, where I would prepare to go to America. I was accepted. Finally, after so many years, my hopes and dreams came true. I was so very happy. It was the biggest accomplishment for me that I had ever dreamed possible. It was only two days later that I said goodbye to the Khao I Dang camp forever, as I made the bus journey to the new camp of Chunbori. On that day, seventeen buses were loaded to transport us to the transit camp, all refugees that had been selected to go to a third country. This was the second convoy of refugees in the RC group that year. My friend, Lim, who was also part of the RC group, was selected by the Americans sometime later. Instead of going to Chonburi, she was sent to Manila for her six months of training before going to America.

Chunbori was the transit camp. People from many neighboring countries would go there before going to America—refugees from Laos, Burma, and Vietnam, as well as Cambodia. It was also the transit camp for all of the others selected to go to other third countries, such as New Zealand, France, Australia, and elsewhere. I was on the American learning track. In the next six months, I learned functional English, in preparing for basic work and living skills. We had to go to school and work each day. At the end of six months, I would be sent with a group by plane to America. While I was in the camp, I learned that I was also given the opportunity to go to France, as the French government had accepted my application as well. But I was very happy with the American choice, so I had no intention of backtracking and changing programs.

My schooling consisted of English for shopping and getting around as well as functional English for basic living skills in America. The language was difficult, being so different from Cambodian, but I worked hard at it. We did woodshop, where I made a table. We had training on how to sew clothing to make our own clothes. We also had a bakery class, which might explain the large number of Cambodian donut shops on the West Coast of the United States, that I later learned about. I never really had the opportunity to go to school in Cambodia, except for a kind of kindergarten and early primary school. The Khmer Rouge did not allow us to have schools, so from the age of nine years, I did not have the chance to study anything in a classroom. However, I had learned plenty of street smarts, surviving the village life, traveling around Cambodia with my friends, and selling and negotiating in the markets.

For work, I did two jobs. One was taking care of children, in a daycare. I worked there with two really nice Thai women supervisors. They did not want me to go, when it was time for me to leave for the next job. The second job was working in an office, making hundreds of Xerox copies for half the day for our school. The Thai people that I worked with were very kind and sweet, very different from the soldiers in the Khao I Dang camp. My attitudes toward Thai people changed dramatically in those six months, as my

94

impression of them was much different in the camp—I honestly met many sweet Thai people during this time.

As my six months came to a close, I began to dream more and more about America. What was it going to be like? The country was so incredibly large. My English was getting better. Although, I was already selected for sponsorship, in the back of my mind, there was a small fear that all of this opportunity could be easily swept away. Everything went smoothly. My life in Chunbori was much better than at Khao I Dang. Many Thai people came into the camp and sold their wares in the Thai market in the center of the camp. It felt more like a small town than a refugee camp, and living conditions were much cleaner and better. Yet, I was still not able to send word to my family from Chunbori to let them know that I was going to America. There was still no agreement between the Thai and Cambodian governments at that time, about exchanging mail. I would have to wait until I reached America.

Quite honestly, I had no idea of what America was really going to be like at all. I had visions of it as being a wealthy country, where life would be much easier. My idea of American cities was that they were a little better than Phnom Penh. There were many more cars in America than in Cambodia, and not many people used bicycles to get around. I was very glad now that I did not get the sponsorship to Malaysia, five years before, when my friend Malradi was accepted to go there. I did receive some letters from Malradi, where he said that he missed me and hoped I would make it to America. He never told me about his job, his family, or really anything, so I did not know very much about his situation. We hoped that one day we would be able to meet up again.

On my last day in the camp, I said goodbye to my friends before leaving. Along with thirty other refugees, we were transported by bus, across Thailand, to Bangkok's airport. We were not allowed to leave our group. We were all too scared to be separated anyway and somehow as a result end up back at Khao I Dang, as punishment. We all stayed close together, as we were passed from the UN officials to security officers in the airport. Our group was divided into smaller groups, as we were all going to different countries. I was in a group of twelve, of which, only five were Cambodian. We eventually made our way to the boarding area of our flight on Thai Airways. I had never been in an airport before, nor had I ever seen a plane so close before on the ground. In fact, I was amazed by the size of the large plane. So many memories flooded through my mind, about my life back in Cambodia, the village life, the killings and starvation, the death fields, my father, my mother, my stepmother, my brother, and my sisters. There were many people in the waiting area from all kinds of ethnic background. My expectations were high. My stomach was beginning to bother me from the intense emotions that were running through my mind.

I was soon to be on my way to America, the place I had fought to go to for so long. Since I was very nervous about the new surroundings, I do not really remember boarding the plane. We were all seated together in the back section of the aircraft. When we took off, I remember feeling very sick, not being used to the aircraft's motion. I could not eat the food they were offering, or drink very much. I was familiar with Coca Cola, because in the past two years, I was able to try it in the camp, when I could purchase it from Thai people who were allowed to bring it into the camp to sell. I was too concerned about what lay before me. I was very excited, but I was wrought with emotion. The plane landed in Narita-Tokyo Airport on the way to America. When we deplaned, we were led upstairs to sit near a cafeteria-style restaurant. From there, we waited for our next departure. UNICEF provided us with food there. We did not have any money to buy anything. Our group stayed in that waiting area for several hours, almost one full day actually, waiting for our connecting flight. From the windows, we could see large jumbo jets everywhere. They were almost like big insects, mainly blue and silver, or with large red tails, slowly moving around the tarmac. Finally, after waiting for what seemed like days, we were taken downstairs to board our plane, to Seattle. I was feeling numb from the combination of excitement, fear of the unknown, and the pain in my heart for leaving my family behind. It was one of the strangest combination of emotions that I had ever felt.

13

THE EMERALD CITY, SEATTLE

I was one of the 2,805 refugees that came to America in 1988 from Cambodia.[3] There were five Cambodians in my group. Only one other Cambodian in my group of five stayed in Seattle, and the rest flew onto Maine. We arrived in Seattle early in the morning on September 22, 1988. I was so sick that I could barely open my eyes to look out the window as we touched down at SEATAC, the international airport for Seattle. I was exhausted, and I had not eaten anything, besides the fried rice that UNICEF provided for me at Narita International Airport in Tokyo. When I stood in line, I was feeling so noticeably sick that they allowed me to move up to the front of the line for the refugees to receive my green card. The inspector asked if my sponsor was planning to meet me at the airport. I told him, "Yes, a family was supposed to pick me up." The inspector told me to come back to see him, if no one was there waiting for me. I was so surprised when I walked into the waiting area when a family that I did not know flashed pictures of me and welcomed me to America. It was my friend Malradi's grandparents that agreed to meet me at the airport. I smiled, but I was not feeling well and I was extremely nervous as I did not know what to expect. They whisked me out to their car,

3 U.S. Committee for Refugees; Refugee Reports, Dec 1987, Dec 1994.

and off we went driving down the highway, away from the airport. It was a rainy, wet morning. They wanted to stop by the grocery store on the way to their home and drive me all over Seattle. It was not long before I suddenly got sick all over the back seat of their car. I was so ashamed, nervous, and tired. I was also not used to riding around in their car. After getting sick, they quickly took me to their home. I was feeling sad and, honestly, disappointed, as their home was very small and cramped. They were kind and welcoming. I appreciated their offer to meet me, to let me stay in their home, and to help me with my expenses until I got situated, even though they really did not have any room for me, which was amazing as they were so generous to help me. As they only had two bedrooms in their home, and the second bedroom was used as a den/storage area, I slept on the floor of their living room, along with their youngest son. I slept there for two days straight, as I was so tired and disoriented. I was happy to eat the food that they offered me. On the same day, they introduced me to the supervisor at Seattle Sewing, in White Center, not far from where they lived.

I began to work there within that week, inspecting clothes that were made there. My English was poor, and I did not understand the Americans at the stores or around White Center very well. There were a few other Cambodians working at that company too. After the first two weeks of working there, I was able to send US$100 to my family through a Cambodian worker's brother who was going back to Battambang to visit relatives. He would deliver the money and a letter to my family. Within a month, I received a letter back, as well as a cassette tape from my family with their recorded voices for me to hear them, telling me about how proud they were that I succeeded in making it to America, and how much they all loved and missed me. I remember my sister Gah (nicknamed "Lye Lye" by that time) crying on the tape. It was the first time that I had heard my family's voices in six years. When I would get home from work, I would listen to the tape over and over, so that I could feel being next to them in some way, and during the lonely times of my initial stay in America, I cried, missing my family so much.

I was feeling strange in White Center. The surroundings did not look all that much better than Sisophon. There was a criminal element to be aware of in White Center, that was different from that in Cambodia. No matter where I was, I was always alert to the potential of theft, but at least it was not the violence or the worry of revolution on a day-to-day basis that I was concerned about in Cambodia. It was overall peaceful. I felt like I had entered a place of a relative safety, yet I knew I had to continue to work hard to save money and figure out a better living situation, not on a living room floor. I actually did not mind sleeping on the floor with a blanket, as that is what I generally did when I was a child before the Khmer Rouge takeover, when I used to sleep in the main living room area alongside my brother, Vuutey.

I was feeling what probably best would be explained as culture shock malaise, as I felt a mixture of anxiety and disappointment at the same time. I did not know at the time that White Center was not exactly one of the best areas in Seattle to live in—actually it was one of the worst. As I had gotten sick on that first day, the Cambodian family was a little hesitant on driving me around Seattle to see other areas.

It was not until three weeks later, when my boss offered to drive me to downtown Seattle, that I was first introduced to the real Emerald City. He drove me downtown in the evening, as the city lights were beginning to turn on. I was shocked. It was unbelievably beautiful, better than I could have ever imagined. *This is what I like,* I thought to myself. Highway 5, back in Sisophon, was much different from the many laned freeway of I-5, running through Seattle. I was amazed as I-5 went right alongside several tall buildings of glass and steel that reached way up into the sky. I had never seen such huge buildings before. All the cars everywhere amazed me as well. There were so many new, modern, and beautiful cars everywhere. I have since learned the make and model of most cars, as it has become a passion of mine. My boss continued to drive me along the freeway. We passed under the Seattle Convention Center, and when we came out the other side of the tunnel underpass, I noticed a really unique building in the distance. From the distance, it looked like a small bowl, surrounded by a ring of lights supported by very long stilts, that were almost as high as the other skyscrapers in the city; that was what my boss called the Space Needle. I was amazed. On the way back, he turned off into the city, so that I could watch people all dressed up walking everywhere. The weather was not cloudy that day, but it was still much cooler than I was used to in Cambodia and Thailand. I had never seen snow before, which I could see in the distance on Mount Rainier. I was so excited after seeing the city. *Yes, I had made a very good choice coming to America,* I thought to myself.

Life was still very difficult, especially with the barriers of language. I was immediately enrolled in South Seattle Community College's ESL program. It was free, as it was offered by the Welfare and Human Services Department in Seattle. I had to take the bus to school and to work. I only stayed with the Cambodian family who had helped to sponsor me for a few weeks. I felt they were very generous to help me, but that they would really like to have their living room back soon. They were truly hoping to sponsor their grandson Malradi who was in Malaysia, and although we were good friends, I was not him. So after a month, I thanked the family profusely for helping me get started and pointing me in the right direction for work, where to buy groceries, and where to avoid places for safety. I moved into a small apartment in White Center. I made only about US$400 per month from my part-time work and welfare assistance. My rent for my small one-bedroom apartment in White Center cost me US$310. The other US$90 per month was divided between food and bus fare. I was never offered food stamps from the welfare services, as I did not qualify. I would buy one chicken and eat from that for the whole week. I would also eat rice and some vegetables but very little fruit. I had to be careful not to overspend, as I would not have enough money for bus fare. I also had to make sure that I always got on the right bus. I was completely on my own. My life was very much like how it was in the refugee camp, living so frugally all of the time, yet life was much more interesting but also in some ways, more frightening. I did not know anyone very well, so I was pretty much all alone, and honestly, quite lonely. After living this way for five or six months, I was very fortunate to be introduced to a very kind Cambodian man, Seim, and his Cambodian wife, Pah. One of my coworkers, Sear, told me about them. So one day, we got in Sear's car and he drove me over to his home to introduce them to me. Seim and Pah liked me immediately and agreed to offer me a room in his house. Seim said, "Well, let's go get your things out of your apartment."

I replied with, "Everything I have is in my backpack, so no need to move anything."

He was in shock, as I was like a kindred spirt, a survivor of the Khmer Rouge, like himself. They were looking for someone to stay with them in their house, to help them with watching their kids during a part of the day. I moved out of my tiny apartment into their home. For the next several years, I lived with them and their two children, Vanna, and Chentah. When Seim and Pah moved to a new house on the edge of Burien and Normandy Park in South Seattle, I moved with them. I had a small room all to myself, and Seim only charged me $200 per month for both rent and food. Pah was an excellent cook, and her way of cooking Cambodian food was very similar to how my mother had cooked for me when I was very young. I appreciated both of them greatly for that. I eventually began to work two jobs, almost sixty hours each week, no longer requiring public assistance, except for the free school, which I also attended. I worked at Seattle Sewing part-time. I also took on a job at the Red Lion hotel, near SEATAC Airport, as a baggage clerk. I also worked in their housekeeping department, where I eventually worked up to answering the phones. Talking with guests as they arrived, I found it an excellent way to practice my English. I saved what money I could, and I sent to my family about US$3,000 over the next four years. When friends would return to the area, near where my family lived, I would give them money to give to my family. This was customary among friends in the Cambodian community in Seattle. My cheap rent and food expense, along with my very busy working schedule, allowed me to save, to build my future.

Seim taught me how to drive soon after moving to Burien. He also introduced me to others in the Cambodian community. I participated in a round robin gift lottery, which helped each of us save up more money quickly. We each contributed US$500. There were twenty of us, and a lucky person who won each month would get the combined amount of what each person contributed. It was based on trust that whoever was holding the money would not run off with the funds, but each of us was trying to establish themselves, so it served everyone's best interest to continue to contribute, even if a person was an early winner. If you already had won, then the prize went to someone who had not won yet. Of course, the last person who won had to wait out the longest for the $10,000 sum. I was able to win after four months, and so with my combined savings, I had more than enough to buy a car. And as soon as I got a driver's license, I was able to buy a car from my savings. No more buses for me. I continued to live with Seim's family, and during this time, I became known to the little kids living with me as Uncle Tha. Seim and Pah became like an uncle and aunt to me. This was Seim's second family, as his former wife and children had all perished during the Khmer Rouge era. I followed Seim's advice, the best that I could, of not spending any money and living frugally. Life was becoming more pleasant, and I was gradually beginning to make ground with my life. Education was very important, as the better I learned English, the more my circumstances improved. Seim and Pah liked having me in their home to help them with watching their kids. I felt, in a way, that I had been adopted into their family. Through them, I came to know many good Cambodians who had also moved to the Burien area, most of whom were property owners there as well, all living the same as Seim, working hard, and living frugally.

For brevity's sake, I will not put too much detail into the first few years of living in America, only that I continued to save, and as my English improved, I was able to make some new and interesting American friends, who took me boating, fishing, hiking, skiing, and sledding around the Pacific Northwest. One particular event which changed my life for the better, which wasn't a great event at the time, was that the first car I purchased was a stick shift. And while I was going around the circular on-ramp to I-509 in Burien, I shifted down instead of up by accident and somehow flipped and rolled my car. I immediately took off my seatbelt and slid out through the back-seat doorway. Luckily, I was mostly uninjured but I was not able to work for a month following the accident while my ribs and other scratches healed. Fortunately, my insurance covered my medical and the cost of a replacement car, which became my Nissan Maxima. During this time off from work, I was able to more frequently visit downtown with my friend Sear, and with other friends, I went to a nightclub called Neighbor's Night Club on Capitol Hill. It was huge, with a big dance floor and great music. On one particular night on July 16, 1992, I met my friend Matt Raudsepp. It was his first night in Seattle, and he was just there trying to figure out the Seattle scene. He had just moved back from teaching English in Japan for two years, and the next day, he was to begin a flight attendant career with a major airline with focus on Asia routes, based in Minnesota. We had fun chatting together, and he was particularly kind and quite interested in Cambodia. He just finished traveling around Asia for a month, most of the time spent in Bali, after Hong Kong and Singapore. He was able to arrange the interview in Seattle with the airline after leaving his job of teaching English in Osaka, Japan. He was offered the job two days prior to our meeting, and he was to start initial training as a flight attendant the next day in Minneapolis. We stayed up all night, and I dropped him off at the Seattle airport the next morning to fly to Minnesota. I never met an American quite like him before, and he almost didn't seem fully Caucasian as he clearly was, because he had spent so much time living in Japan and traveling to parts of the Far East. So with the help of a friend, I wrote a short message on a card and mailed it to him while he was at his training in Minneapolis.

Shortly after he began flying, he got a layover in Seattle, so the day before he planned to arrive in Seattle, he called Seim's house. Luckily, I was home to take his call, and I told him that I would meet him and drive him around the city. So, we made the plan. It was the beginning of a great friend-ship, and to this day, we are still best friends. During his visit, I brought him to my house in Burien to meet with Seim and Pah. Matt really took to them, and he was amazed by Seim and Pah's life story, and from what I could tell him about my family story as well. Matt's family lived in Oregon, not anywhere close to Seattle. I dropped him off at his hotel, and we made plans for him to travel on his pass travel benefit to see me on his upcoming days off. He was based in Memphis when he started, but he knew that eventually he would go to the Seattle or Honolulu bases when positions opened up, because of his Japanese language skills. I would get confused with my English, calling Memphis "Mempolis" as I would get it confused with Minneapolis. America was a huge country with so many different city names, so I frequently confused them.

The airlines have planes that not only go up and down, but they have their economic cycles which go up and down as well. After only four months into his new job transitioning from Osaka to Minneapolis, and finally to Memphis, Matt found himself furloughed with all the other new flight attendants hired during the summer, so he asked Seim and Pah if he could stay with us all in Seattle. Seim gladly accepted. Matt found a job working at the front desk of the Seattle Westin Hotel. He greeted Japanese guests when there was a language barrier, and he ended up working in their premier check-in area for VIP guests. It was a good time for us to get to know each other well, to help each other out financially, and to explore the Pacific Northwest as well. We decided that year to get an apartment together, as we needed more room. So with mixed emotions, we moved out from Seim and Pah's house, and into an apartment nearby. After one year, Matt was recalled to his airline, and he commuted to Boston for a few months, until he was able to get into the Seattle base. He commuted to Seattle and kept a "flight attendant pad" in Winthrop near the Boston Logan Airport with sixteen other flight attendants during his commuting time. I began working at a new job at a company in Ballard that made textile products for Boeing and the military.

Matt and I continued to live together and explore the areas around Seattle, making various friends. Seim found a little house in early 1995, and we decided to buy it together. Matt was out flying a trip, when we made the offer. Yet Seim decided to sell his half percentage to Matt, so we owned the house and fixed it up together as an investment in Burien. It was a very different situation, to own one's own home. It was very stable for both of us, as a way to build a foundation and save. We got to meet our neighbors, and our next door neighbor, Charlie, a retired school teacher, really took to us. We worked a lot in the garden areas outside the small house, and we had all kinds of flowers growing, and we planted different flowering trees. I felt very safe and secure for the first time in my life. I was also encouraged by Matt and Charlie to begin studying for the US citizenship test. Matt made cassette tapes for me and my Cambodian friends to study the questions and helped us memorize the questions and answers. Everyone was given questions ahead of time to study. So one of my greatest achievements ever was finally attaining my American citizenship on October 27, 1995, seven years after being in America. I no longer had to rely on my green card. But most importantly, it had more meaning than I can express in words, giving me the solid foundation to build my future in a country that is so rich with opportunity. Many of my closest friends celebrated with me, including Matt. Marion and John, who had become like adoptive American parents to me, and their son, James, insisted on treating me and some of my friends to dinner that night. I have always appreciated their kindness in looking out for me and their worrying over me as well at times. My adoptive Cambodian family, Seim and Pah, also had a celebration for me at their home.

Among other opportunities, Matt had flight benefits which he could share with me as a traveling companion, so he invited me along on a few of his family visits, and on other trips to various places around the United States. He enjoyed taking me with him on trips and showing me America. In those early days, I was lucky enough to go to Hawaii multiple times, as well as Reno, San Francisco, and New York, for very little cost, on his companion passes. Matt, who had taught English in Japan for two years prior to being a flight attendant, was also able to help me with my English studies. His mom, Rosalie, was a second grade teacher, so she helped me as well.

In 1995, Matt even tried to help me go back to Cambodia, through Tokyo and Bangkok on a travel pass, but due to unforeseen circumstances, while enroute to Tokyo, the connecting flight to Bangkok filled up, and being

February, a difficult month to travel in Asia due to the Chinese New Year, we were not able to travel standby to any neighboring country, where we could buy another ticket to Siem Reap or Phnom Penh. At the layover hotel in Tokyo, Matt and another friend of his, Brett, who just happened to be on working layover there, spent several hours going through the computer to find any possible combination of cities to travel through to get even to Bangkok from Tokyo-Narita Airport. The only two options were to either go to Singapore and take the train up through the Malaysian peninsula to Bangkok, but all the return flights out of Singapore, Bangkok, and even Hong Kong were all sold out for the next month, and the second choice was to do another Hawaiian trip, leaving the next evening on the red-eye back to Hawaii from Tokyo. As traveling standby seemed too tenuous at that time, we could not risk getting stuck in Thailand and having to pay an immediate full-fare ticket to get home, costing us a great deal during the Chinese New Year time, so we opted for the second choice of another Hawaiian vacation. My friend Matt was very sad that he could not help me get back home on one of his passes. I tried not to show my disappointment, but he knew well that I was very disappointed on the inside. I really wanted to see my family again so badly, yet I had to be wise to this road block. I began to feel that there might have been a reason for all the obstacles that we faced in going back to Cambodia at that time. Actually, as it turned out, our plan for me to hire a taxi to go and get my family to bring them to the Thai side of the border for a reunion at the crossover point near Aranyaprathet and Poipet probably would not have worked out anyway. It was better that we did not try to go that far and fail, or discover that the area was unsafe. It was a little naive to think that we could have met them in that way anyway. There was no sense taking the risk. It would be better to buy a regular ticket next time and fly directly into Phnom Penh or Siem Reap from somewhere in Asia and for us to stay far away from the border crossing areas and make the plans very clear and simple in the future.

As it turned out, the border crossing between Thailand and Cambodia ended up being closed for a duration due to Khmer Rouge skirmishes from some hold-out groups in the countryside. It still was not completely safe. Landmines were getting cleared completely throughout the border areas from large donations around the world through the UN, Red Cross, and UNESCO. We did end up having a nice trip in Hawaii, where we stayed in both Kona and Honolulu. The weather was very much like that of Cambodia, only cooler with less humidity. It was on this trip that Matt and I decided to start putting my story in writing for others to learn from it. Many people have never heard of Cambodia or of the atrocities that had happened there.

The nice thing about flying with Matt was that we were able to fly in business class on passes through his job benefit, which made the long distance flying much easier to take. Matt knew the flight crew as well, as he had just worked the flight from Tokyo-Narita to Seattle the day before as the purser (flight leader). So the crew doted on me. I was not used to that kind of attention or special treatment. Other passengers kept looking at me, wondering if I were someone famous. On the way to Honolulu from Tokyo, he did not know the crew, as it was not his normal route, but we were still spoiled. We sat at seats 1A and 1B on the main level, right in the nose, below the cockpit of the 747. It was around 7:00 a.m. when we arrived in Honolulu. We decided to visit the main island, so we flew on to Kona from there. On our return from Kona, we stayed in Waikiki for just a couple of days, so that we would have enough time to make it back home, before we both had to report to work. I loved to tell Matt, "I grew up in a mudhole but now I am flying in first class."

The best thing about the trip was that the adventure really got my mind off of work and I was doubly thankful to finally arrive home with a renewed appreciation of everything that I had built up over the recent years. I still wanted to see my family, but I knew that I would go back sooner than later, and flying to Tokyo the previous week made me realize that I could honestly return home to see them, but maybe in a year or so, when the security was better and the border would not be closed down so frequently for flights in and out of Cambodia.

During the following summer, I began to ponder about the many struggles in my life, and I realized that I had finally achieved a sense of security and a sense of peace, like wading to shore or to the shallows from a turbulent ocean. And the beach that I had found was even more beautiful and tranquil than the exotic white and yellow sand beach of Koh Kong, where I went swimming with my friends so many years ago in Cambodia, My house was very small and non-descript, but it was safe. Yet, I felt it was time to do something for my family, and I was not sure yet what to do. I decided to put my mind toward saving up all of the money that I could in the next year so that I could return on my own early in the following year to see my family again. Over the years of living in America, I had purchased different gifts that I had hoped to one day give to my sisters, brother, and father upon returning. I missed them terribly, and I needed to go back to my roots to be with them again, to see my old home in Sisophon. I missed my father, who was getting very advanced in his years, especially for the war-torn Cambodia. I hoped that I would be able to see him before too much time passed. I have carried, in some ways, a sense of guilt for not being able to help my family more, and from my decision to come to America in my adolescence, with all the risks it entailed. Yet, I felt it was the best choice, as the political situation in Cambodia seemed so unstable. I would never go back to that awful village that the Khmer Rouge enslaved me to live in. I never wanted to be at their mercy again. Yet, I also wanted to see my sisters, Pah, Paht, Met, and Gah (Lye-Lye), as well as my brother, Vuutey. I had learned from letters, that had been brought back with friends, that all of them had married. I desperately wanted to go back to see them yet also wanted to stay safe and retain my life in Seattle. Luckily, in the previous two years, the northwest corner of Cambodia, where my family lived, was no longer as dangerous to visit as it had been. So it was with great excitement, as well as trepidation, that I planned my trip back home.

14

THE TRIP BACK HOME,
MARCH 31, 1997

The day of my departure arrived. My friends, Matt and Seim, saw me off at the airport. As we stood in line waiting to check my luggage, I glimpsed at the others around me who were traveling to Japan, or to other countries beyond. Everyone had a similar sense of excitement and anticipation. As my bags were tagged PNH for Phnom Penh, and my seat assignment was confirmed, the realization struck me that my ticket was no longer merely a piece of paper and that shortly, I would be boarding the first flight of my journey back to Cambodia. I had no idea of what to expect once I finally made my way all the way back to Battambang, the provincial region of my hometown. Cambodians that I knew who were from that area made the trip back home in the past year without difficulty to see their family. For years, the northwestern region of Cambodia was not safe, as the Khmer Rouge continued on with their skirmishing in that area. For the time being, the fighting had subsided. Although the two co-premiers in the government were at odds with each other and the capital city had just experienced a labor protest the day before, where grenades had been thrown into the crowds killing seventeen workers and injuring many more, I hoped that Cambodia would be safe enough for my return.

In the south satellite of SEATAC International Airport, while sitting and talking with Matt and Seim in the boarding area near our departure gate, a couple of flight attendants passing by, from the Osaka-bound flight crew, recognized Matt and came over to talk with us. Matt introduced Seim and me to them, and they wished me luck on my return trip after Matt explained to them that I was returning home to visit after being away from my family for many years. It was a nice distraction from my busy thinking, to meet some very friendly coworkers of his, before they boarded their working trip to Japan.

As I wanted to get underway to begin my adventure back home, the waiting time in the airport seemed interminable. Finally, the boarding announcements were made, and it was time for me to say goodbye to my friends and to move in the general direction of the boarding door. I waved goodbye, as I looked back from the jetway's entrance one last time. Matt and Seim were watching me from behind the crowd that was waiting for me to board. As I boarded the plane, I remembered how different everything had been from boarding the plane years before when coming to America. I had become much more sure of myself in recent years. This flight would also be much easier as I brought along my CD player, magazines, and books as well. As the immense plane eventually pushed back from the gate, and the safety video played over the movie screens, I was filled with emotion, almost disbelieving that I might just see my family in days, not in years, as I had become conditioned to accept, over the past fourteen years.

Matt had given my picture to another friend of his, who would be working on the first flight of my journey to Tokyo. She usually flew the purser position, and so he hoped that she would pass around my picture to the crew during their predeparture briefing. She captured the attention of the crew with my picture and the attached note, mentioning the circumstances of my return trip back to Cambodia. Later, onboard the plane, the entire crew did their best to go out of their way to do extra for me on the flight. The Japanese woman who sat next to me on the plane shyly asked me if I were someone famous, as most of the fourteen flight attendants onboard came up to me, one by one, to introduce themselves to me at various times throughout the flight when I was not submerged under my blanket. I was made to feel very comfortable, like a king, on the first ten-hour leg of my journey.

The journey to reach Phnom Penh, via Tokyo-Narita Airport and Bangkok, took three days, counting the lost day, due to passing over the international date line. For the first leg of my journey from Seattle to Tokyo, the afternoon seemed to linger at 3:00 p.m., as the sun's light did not diminish for the entire ten-hour flight. It was a strange illusion, that seemed to extend my quick farewell to my friends in Seattle for a few hours, as the plane traveled in the same direction as the sun, in its westward trajectory. It did not seem like time was passing until the in-flight movie began to mark the passage of time. We arrived at Tokyo-Narita Airport the following day at about 4:50 p.m., although we never experienced darkness, as is the case when traveling west over the date line during the daytime.

My transit in Tokyo was simple and easy, and I only waited an hour at the airport, before boarding my connecting flight to Bangkok. The change of flights, taking me deeper into the Far East, precipitated my growing excitement. In only another seven hours after take-off from Tokyo, I would be back in Thailand, where I would wait for my final transfer to my flight to Phnom Penh. At about the time my plane left Tokyo for Bangkok, it was 6:00 p.m., Tokyo time, although it was then 2:00 a.m. in Seattle, the day before. On the second flight from Tokyo to Bangkok, the plane continued to travel toward the west, but in a much more southwesterly direction. The plane no longer traveled in the close alignment with the sun, as the plane had done on the previous flight. Daylight continued for just a couple of more hours, until the sun could finally be seen setting in the far distance from my window. As a result, it seemed like a very long afternoon, although my body clock was eventually registering the middle of the night. I was still functioning on Pacific Standard Time, in Seattle. I was becoming increasingly tired, and for most of the second flight, I slept, not paying any attention to the in-flight movies that were showing, or the food that was being offered.

The plane touched down in Bangkok at about midnight, or about 10:00 a.m. Seattle time. Despite my grogginess, I had an amazing amount of energy, considering the many hours of sitting on the plane. It was midnight in Bangkok, so of course it was late, but in Seattle, it was mid-morning. I pulled myself off my seat and rechecked to make sure that my gold chains in my shirt pocket and around my neck, were still intact, and that my money belt, with American passport, was still snugly in place under my pants. I made my way off the plane and to the transit area. A few shops were still open, even at that late hour at the airport. I planned to stay at the Bangkok airport overnight, as my flight to Phnom Penh left early the following morning. The airport was open twenty-four hours, and it was perfectly safe, as long as I kept a careful watch on my belongings. Many others, who were also transiting, stayed at the airport overnight as well so that they would not have to go through customs and immigration in Thailand. During the night, I ran into a group of Cambodians traveling together, who were enroute from a study tour in Paris. They welcomed me to sit near them to help me pass the time conversing in Cambodian. It was interesting to see that Cambodia was developing enough, once again, to have students study abroad, not that I would have considered such an idea for myself if I had continued with my old life of trading in Cambodia years before. They were interested in hearing about where I had been living, but I felt a little shameful, as they were so much more educated than me.

Finally, it was time to leave for Phnom Penh. The sun was now up in the east. I thought about my friends back in Seattle and my garden at my Seattle home. My mind wandered to thoughts of the adventure just ahead. As my plane gained speed, taking off for the last leg of my long journey, I immediately drifted off to sleep, and I was no longer aware of where I was, until I was awakened by the sudden bump of the tires hitting the ground, an hour later, in Phnom Penh. My eyes opened to reveal to me, from the window near my seat, a sunny morning in my native country of Cambodia.

Immigration and customs were surprisingly simple and uncomplicated, aside from the fact that Cambodian soldiers with machine guns were standing guard. I purchased a thirty-day visa at immigration, and I quickly passed through customs. In the arrivals area, all around me, I was accosted by taxi drivers and other tour promoters. One of my Cambodian friend's brothers was holding up a sign with my name on it, so I could locate him. My friend's brother was also named Tha, his full name being Tha In (Tah Een) Tha In's parents were also there to greet me on my arrival. When we walked out of the air-conditioned airport, into the open Cambodian air, the intense heat and high humidity hit me, like walking into a sauna from a refrigerator. They quickly guided me over to where their car was parked, and we loaded up the car with my luggage. It was 1:00 p.m. when we left the airport for my hotel, in Tha In's '86 model, Toyota Corolla.

From the windows, I was amazed with the changes that I saw, as the car drove away from the airport in the direction of the city. There were many American oil companies represented there with their gas stations along the highway. There were cars everywhere—it was a much different Phnom Penh than I remembered. There were billboards advertising Toyota and Honda cars, as well as a wide variety of cigarettes. Famous Cambodian actors and actresses were featured in many of the different advertisements along the roadway in the city. Cambodian writing was everywhere. A Mercedes even passed us by. The weather was extremely hot and humid, much different from the mild climate that I had become accustomed to in Seattle. They drove me to my hotel, which cost me only US$25 per night. It was luxurious by any standard.

With the growing excitement from being back in my native country, I could not let myself sleep even after being on the plane for hours. The family asked me if I would like to go to dinner. I readily agreed, replying with, "Take me somewhere cheap, cheap." I was thinking that I ought to save my money at the time, still thinking in American terms of "cheap." So off we went to a "cheap, cheap place" in central Phnom Penh. Dinner was certainly inexpensive at the place they chose, about fifty cents per person to eat there. Aside from being cheap, there was no air-conditioning in the almost 105°F city heat and 80 percent humidity. There was just a big fan that did an excellent job of blowing around the hot, stinky air from the restaurant. Along with the air, the fan also blew around more flies than I could have ever imagined being in one room at the same time. I did not eat the food that I ordered for the fear of getting sick. Going to such a "cheap, cheap" place was a bad idea for sure, as I could not handle the shock of it. Tha In's family was worried that I was not feeling well. I politely explained to them that it was the jetlag that ruined my appetite. They were eating heartily, as I tried to keep myself cool sitting close to the fan. I was dripping wet from perspiration in just a few minutes of being in that place. Eventually we left, and they were very grateful for me picking up the tab of about US$3.

After that, Tha In dropped me off at my hotel, so that he could take his parents' home. I had about an hour and a half to settle into my room, before he came back to pick me up. I was beginning to really feel the weariness setting in, yet I needed to search for a plane ticket for my final flight to Battambang Airport, located very near to Sisophon. When Tha In returned, we immediately set out to find a travel agency. At first, we thought it would be easy, but we ended up going to about five different places in the city before we could find a ticket. As the Cambodian New Year was approaching (April 13th), all the plane tickets had been booked well in advance. I did not want to go by train, or by ship, as I was carrying so many gifts to give to everyone. I was not familiar with the changes in the country, so I did not feel safe in taking an indirect route to Battambang. We finally found a travel agent who had a ticket, which had been returned just a few hours before. Unfortunately, the departure was not set for another four days. I decided to take it anyway, as I did not know if I would be able to find another ticket soon. Exhaustion was beginning to set in, as the heat and the lack of sleep were taking their toll. I returned to my hotel and slept.

The next day I went out in search of my friend Succun. I eventually found his old home on the west side of Phnom Penh, where his mother now lived. Everyone in their family was so shocked to see me. I also revisited

Malradi's family briefly on the day before my flight to Battambang. I found his family's old home right across the street from the city stadium, not far from the Olympic Market, just as everything had been before. Malradi's mother cried when she saw me, thanking me for being such a wonderful friend to her son in the camp. They had no idea of what had become of me, as they had lost word of me, and I did not have their address to write to them. She said that if it were not for me, Malradi would have never made it across the border and he would not have survived so much in the camp. She told me that he would never have found as trustworthy a friend as me. Also, had he not met me, he would still be in Cambodia till that very day, or even worse. She wanted me to stay for dinner with their family, but I saw that they were very busy with their shop on the first floor of their home. I did not want to take them away from their business, or to be any trouble for them. After getting Malradi's current phone number in Malaysia, I bid them all farewell. I was very happy to see some of my old friends, but my focus was on seeing my family. If it were at all possible, I would have grown wings to fly myself to Sisophon right then.

Finally, the moment I had long waited for arrived. It was now time to board the Air Cambodge flight to Battambang. The plane, although it had air-conditioning, was still quite hot. I sweat so much that it is embarrassing. I did not want to draw attention to myself, as I was carrying a good amount of money and jewelry with me, to give to my family. It was still so amazing to see Cambodians all around me. Of course, I was used to the homogeneity of my country while growing up, but after living in America for nine years, I had become used to seeing so many different kinds of people. In some respects, I felt like a stranger in my own land. In the past several days, even my dreams were filled with Cambodian people, not the multiethnic American people that filled my dream images in my sleep back home in America.

The flight lasted only thirty minutes. As soon as we reached a level altitude, I could see the rice paddy fields in all directions. Battambang's primary industry has always been rice cultivation. It felt so amazing to be going back, like a dream. But I knew it wasn't a dream, as I began to feel sick, from the rocky plane. It smelled like a mixture of Pine-Sol cleaning solution and jasmine tea. Jasmine tea and water was offered onboard, which I did not want to think about at the moment. I honestly had no idea how my family was, and whether my father was still alive. I was getting excited about seeing my family, but I was also growing nervous, as I did not know what to expect. The last time that I had been able to talk to my family was a year and a half ago on the telephone. After sending them some money through a Cambodian family's personal business, my family was brought to the phone to confirm that they had received the money. My father did not sound very coherent, and the connection was poor. It was from a public telephone that they had called me. They did not have a phone in their home. I sent a letter to both my father and elder sister, about a month ago, to let them know that I was coming, but I did not know if they had received my letters yet. It was entirely possible that they had no idea that I was coming. It was my plan, once in Battambang, to check into a hotel and to hire a taxi to drive to Sisophon, to find my brother, Vuutey, and eldest sister, Pah, and to have them brought back to my hotel. I did not want to go to Sisophon by myself, as I did not know about the area's safety.

Immediately after arriving in Battambang and picking up my luggage, I looked outside, around the arrivals area, to hire a taxi. Several taxi drivers approached me at first, but unlike the drivers in Phnom Penh, they did not fight for my attention. The driver who approached me first, luckily, seemed like a good enough choice, but I certainly would not trust him enough to tell him that I did not know my way around Battambang. I did not want anyone to know that I was returning from America, so I told the taxi driver that I was from Phnom Penh. If I told him the truth, he might suspect me of carrying a great deal of money, which I was. I paid him US$5 for the ride to the hotel. I told him to take me to the Semaki Hotel, a hotel that a friend in Seattle recommended to me. The driver insisted on taking me to International Hotel, which he claimed was much better. I relented, and as it turned out, I was quite happy about his choice. I decided to hire him to make the trip to Sisophon to pick up my family. We agreed on US$40 for the 120-kilometer round trip. Since I did not know about the current situation in the province, I did not want to trust a stranger to take me alone over the sixty kilometers of rough roads. I could be mugged and left somewhere in the bushes. There may also be problems with bandits or soldiers along the way, although the Khmer Rouge threat seemed long passed since. I felt it was better to pay for a taxi to pick up my family and bring them to meet me.

I figured that it would probably take four hours for him to drive there and back over the rough roads, so I gave my clothes over for cleaning once I checked into my room. It only cost me fifty cents to have my clothes cleaned. People stared at me in the lobby of the hotel. They could tell that I was not from around there. Unbelievably, there were also four American guys in their twenties in the lobby, talking in English. I knew they were from America, because of their accent. I couldn't believe it. There they were, all casually dressed in T-shirts and shorts, ready to go out sight-seeing just the same as if they had gone to any other city. I was too shy to ask them where they were from, and I was afraid of advertising the fact that I was returning to see my family. A street-smart person would realize that I was probably carrying money or other expensive gifts with me. It did not want anyone to overhear, or for myself to necessarily join up with their group, as I might be invited to do so. Just the way I spoke Cambodian made the front desk staff ask me where I was from. I just smiled and told them that I was from Phnom Penh. I decided that once I got to my room, I would stay there. I would just wait for the taxi to return.

I sat in my shorts while I relaxed and waited in the room. The room I was staying in was surprisingly nice, especially for just US$10 per night. The room was much more spacious than my room in Phnom Penh, with high ceilings, two large double beds, and brand new furnishings. The room had just been newly remodeled, and the floor had beautiful tile, forming the picture of a flower arrangement. The room was also secure. I had a nice view from the second floor of the market across the street. Strangely enough, the name of the market was "Nuts Market" in English. I thought to myself, *Why would anyone name a market after crazy people?* Or maybe it was a foreboding sign about my decision to return home. I left my traveling suitcase in Phnom Penh with Tha In's family. The giant roller-bag that I brought over in cargo stood in the middle of the room in front of me. I had brought about 120 shirts, several pairs of pants, and children's clothes that included little dresses, little toddler shirts, and short pants for my nieces and nephews. Apart from the clothes, money, and knickknacks for gifts, I also brought gold chains and necklaces that could be melted down in time of need for my family. I hoped that I had brought enough to give something significant to everyone. I only brought a couple of change of clothes for myself, and that was it, except for my amenity bag. *Maybe I WAS NUTS*, I thought to myself, *attempting to return home with so much to give to my family.*

I took a hot bath, while I waited and relaxed. I was so hot and sweaty from being around outside. It was April, the hottest month of the year in Cambodia, and it was very hot and humid outside. I was very happy to have air-conditioning in my room. I had a Mitsubishi TV with remote, which I later flicked on from the bed to peruse the channels. I looked for CNN, and I could not believe what program I found in English first. It seemed almost incredulous that on TV in Battambang, I was watching Oprah Winfrey. It was amazing to think of how things had developed so much in my absence, to be able to not only watch television but to also be able to view shows from the United States. It was being broadcasted on the Jakarta station and was received from the hotel's satellite dish on the roof of the hotel. I surfed channels some more and discovered some different Indian and Thai stations, as well as a station broadcasting from Phnom Penh. Three were news programs in a multitude of languages, as well as dancing and other multicultural soaps. I quickly drifted off to sleep.

I woke up from my nap suddenly, from the pounding on the door of my hotel room. I quickly jumped out of bed to look out the window to see who was there. I saw a police car and soldiers with machine guns outside. "Oh no, what is happening?" In front of the police car was parked a taxi. I was not sure that it was the taxi that I had hired to pick up my family. With groggy eyes, and a feeling of alarm, I tried to get my mind focused to think clearly.

I was expecting my family about this time. The pounding continued on the door and I began to fear after being jolted awake that I could be in imminent danger of soldiers breaking into my room and taking away my money. "Who is it?" I asked in English. There was no response and the pounding continued, which made my heart pound louder and louder too. I said again, "Who is it?" At that moment, from the window, I noticed the taxi's back door open. I saw my sister and another woman get out, helping a very old and frail man out of the car. It was my father! "Oh, my God!" I said to myself in English. A million feelings rushed through my mind all at once. I then heard the voice of the taxi driver say in English, "It is your brother." In Cambodian, I heard, "*Knee Bahng. Knee Bahng!* [It's your brother!] *Baktweah Own!* [Please open the door, younger brother!]" A new feeling that I honestly never felt before, filled my heart, a feeling beyond happiness and joy, realizing that yes, I was going to see my family after so long. I quickly went to the door, unlatched it, and flung it open. My brother, Vuutey, was standing there with open arms. Soon, my father and sisters had made it up the stairs, to the second floor, and they were coming down the hall. No one spoke at first, because of the shock, and then everyone cried with happy tears and smiles.

My brother told me to bow to my father there in the opening of the doorway. In the Cambodian tradition, I got down on my knees, with my hands in prayer form just below my chin. I bowed forward three times, not less than three, and not more than three, to show my father the proper respect. I was never so happy in my life. Never. To be able to see my family again after so long, it was the greatest joy that I ever had in my life. My mind was racing with millions of thoughts, remembrances, and questions. "Why did I ever leave, in the first place?" "What was better than family?" I was overcome with emotion.

My family all came into the room. Among those who came were my father, Jaik, my brother, Vuutey, and my brother's wife, Toll, my sister, Pah, Pah's husband, Hey, and my sister's son, Tear. Vuutey said, "Let's go now, so we can get home before dark." I explained to them that my clothes were all being washed and that they had not been returned yet. My brother said, "Wear your shirt wet, as it won't matter outside anyway." I ran up the six flights of stairs to retrieve my clothes. Although they had not been dried completely and ironed, I paid both of the housekeepers US$2, because I was so excited about seeing my family. I was too excited to feel embarrassed about not wearing my shirt. They were very surprised as US$2 was a great deal of money for them, and they had not even finished cleaning my clothes yet. I put my clothes in a bag and I ran back downstairs. Meanwhile, my brother-in-law, Hey, had left and returned to tell my sister, Gah, now called "Lye Lye" that I had come back home. I was surprised that he had returned to the hotel so quickly. I asked him, "How did you get back so quickly?" He responded by telling me that Lye Lye now lived only two blocks from the hotel where I was staying. I could not believe it that for the entire time I was waiting, I could have met her as she lived so close. My younger sister cried terribly after learning that I was there, but she wouldn't be able to spend time with me that afternoon, as we had to leave right away to get to Sisophon before dark. Vuutey explained that it was dangerous at night. It was Lye Lye who was the last of my family to say goodbye to me, before I left for Thailand with my friend, Malradi, years before. Everything happened so quickly. We were not in the hotel more than twenty-five minutes together, before I was able to gather up all of my belongings and dresses and be checked-out.

A different driver took us back to Sisophon, a friend of the other taxi driver. The first driver had already made a small fortune for himself that day, from receiving so much in American currency. The average monthly pay in that part of Cambodia was US$30 per month. For one day's work, he made US$45, minus the cost of the tank of gas. I paid the hotel clerk the full US$10 for my stay, although I did not stay through the night. Curious eyes watched my family and me as we left. I was surprised now by the soldiers that I had previously seen from the window but forgot about after seeing my father. Vuutey explained that he had become the general manager of the police in that region, and so following our taxi was a car with four soldiers with machine guns, for protection.

The white '87 model Toyota Camry drove us through the streets of Battambang, toward the outskirts of the city. It was strange to be in such a fairly nice car, so far into the rural areas of Cambodia. Battambang was the second largest city in Cambodia, but it seemed odd that the city had developed so much in the past fourteen years. Around us were other older Japanese cars, people on bicycles, and cycles, as well as pedestrians carrying food and other items from the market. We traveled down a street of *rumdul trees* that I remembered going to with my mother when I was a child. The trees were well known for being very large and old, one or two hundred years old, and having beautiful white flowers. Birds would stay in the trees to hide in the shade of the branches during the intense heat of the afternoon sun. It was interesting to also look at the buildings of Battambang now and to compare them to the buildings of America. Battambang was still a very old city, with many brick buildings, never reaching above three stories. The city had an appeal though, as it was kept fairly clean and there was activity everywhere. I did not recall so many buildings and so many store fronts on the first floor of many homes in the city as well. Still there was a great deal of poverty, but business enterprise was also thriving. On the radio, a sad Cambodian song played, which was so amazingly fitting to the moment, with the words saying, "Welcome home."

Despite the air-conditioning in the car, I was so hot. I was not used to the intense heat. My family took advantage of all available space in the vehicle, as five squeezed into the back seat together with my father in the middle. Vuutey's young son, Oun, of about five years old, sat on my lap in the front seat with me. He was excited about meeting me, but he really did not understand who I was, or where I had come from. The car bounced so much over the badly maintained roads that my father said, "I think my shirt is going to break!"

It took us only ten minutes to clear the city streets to Highway 5 that led its way toward Sisophon. The road was terrible with giant potholes everywhere. It was certainly not the smooth freeway that I was used to in America. My sister Pah leaned forward, reaching over my seat to massage my upper back and neck and to wipe the sweat from my face with her handkerchief. Everyone talked and asked so many questions. While riding in the car, they told me about how they were so surprised when the taxi came to the village. When my father learned that I had sent for only Vuutey and Pah to come to Battambang, he began to cry. And although he could not really walk, he got up and tried moving toward the car, because he wanted to see me so badly, afraid that I would not make the journey all the way to Sisophon. So Vuutey and Pah, of course, helped him into the taxi. Since Vuutey decided to also bring his police car, everyone who was present piled into the car, along with the four police officers who accompanied him. It was remarkable to be home after so long, and after so much. I was not sixteen anymore, the age when I left, but thirty now. They still recognized me, although I was not the skinny boy they remembered. They wondered what I ate in America that made me so large. I was not fat, of course, just fit and well-nourished. My father told me that he had been saving the pants and shirt that he was wearing for the day of my return. I had made them for him twenty years before.

The drive along Highway 5 was also interesting, and I was so glad for the air-conditioner. From the windows, we could look into the intense heat outside, and the high humidity, and know we were somewhat protected inside the car. We drove by many rice fields, and occasionally small clusters of huts. During the hour-and-a-half car ride, my family asked me if I wanted any food. Although I was hungry, I told them not to stop but to continue on our way to Sisophon. I came too far to wait anymore to see my hometown village in the suburbs of Sisophon again. The surroundings began to look familiar again, and then it was another sense of sheer bewilderment as we finally drove up to the area where my boyhood home once stood. Except for Vuutey's house, none of the houses were made from wood, as they were during my boyhood, but instead, they were all made from wooden poles and thatched coconut palms.

Many nieces and nephews came to the car, along with other curious neighbors, to greet me. My sister Pah wanted to take my shoes off for me when I entered the house. I felt so embarrassed by all their attention. They told me that they would make a special Cambodian dinner for me. They were curious as to what I ate in America, and if I had eaten any Cambodian dishes recently. I told them that in Seattle. there were a couple of Cambodian grocery stores, where I would buy special Cambodian ingredients to cook at home. They were surprised.

I stayed in my brother's home. His family home was right near the train station stop, only 200 meters from the land where my boyhood home stood while growing up. His house was now the closest to the train station of many homes that were there now, as he had expanded his home extensively to also have a restaurant on its first floor. The train station was in better shape than in the years following the Vietnamese takeover, but it was still not as nice as it was from my early boyhood days, before the Khmer Rouge. Vuutey's house was divided into two sections. A restaurant made up the front section, which was mainly a large kitchen. In the front of the house on a patio were several tables and chairs for customers to sit and eat. In this section, there was also a place where Cambodian guests could rest inside, on rice mats, while they waited for the train. On another side of the house was a small booth that they rented out to people on a daily basis that sold pharmaceutical products such as toothbrushes and soap. Toilet paper was a popular item that was usually sold there. In the main section of the house, where Vuutey's family lived, there were several small rooms, and a second story. The house had indoor plumbing, which I did not have while growing up. Customers were not present at the restaurant or in the little store, as the one train leaving for Battambang left at about 2:00 p.m., several hours before. It was then close to 7:00 p.m. Very few people came by the home in the evenings.

It was so wonderful to be back home, to be with my family again. I felt as if the whole world was standing still or that nothing else mattered to me than to just be there with them. I had no idea of what to expect before my visit. I did not know if my father was still alive, and how my family, in general, was doing. I also worried that my brother had hard feelings toward me for leaving the family so many years ago. For several years in America, I sometimes wondered if my brother hated me because of my decision to leave, despite everyone's trepidations, but once seeing my brother again, I knew that my feelings were totally unfounded. It was only because they all loved me so much that they did not want me to be hurt or separated again. A sense of calmness filled my heart for the first time in so long. I felt a well spring of energy on seeing my family again. It was a place of perfect belonging that I had craved in these past years. The tumultuous waters had washed me to shore. I felt as if I had finally arrived, after so long. My mind and heart were at peace.

15

REUNITING WITH MY FAMILY, 1997

For the next several days, I stayed with my family and celebrated. We all ate well, and it was the best New Year's celebration that I had ever had. On the first night, my sister-in-law cooked *dreyross*, a big fish with very few bones—the most expensive fish that is served in Cambodia. Paht was there as well, along with several nieces and nephews, for dinner. We were up very late, until at least 1:00 a.m., that first night. I had no desire to sleep, although I was terribly tired from all the traveling and the intense heat of the day. I tried to explain as well as I could of what life was like in America, and how I lived there, with my day-to-day routine, of commuting to work by car for sixteen miles each morning, and having two days off each week. Everything I said to them seemed so remote and hard to understand. I was feeling so tired that I felt that I was both sleeping and talking at the same time. My little nieces and nephews, of around three to six years old, crawled all over me while I talked.

Tear, my eldest nephew of twenty-one years, remembered me from his early boyhood. He always found his way to sit right next to me during my entire stay. He was married with a baby already. He was very curious and liked trying to use my camcorder. June, my second eldest nephew, was seventeen. He was also very curious and followed me around constantly during my stay, although he was quite shy. Tear was born in the Khmer Rouge village. I remember from before the stories that Pah told me about her baby son in the village.

She had been so malnourished that she was unable to provide any natural milk to Tear when he was a baby. They improvised by letting him suck rice soup instead. Amazingly, he survived the malnourishment that everyone had suffered through in the Khmer Rouge village. June was born to Paht, after she had returned to Sisophon, so he was very lucky to miss the holocaust completely.

My father was a very proud man, with so many grandchildren. I now had thirty-two nieces and nephews. My father sat and listened quietly as so many questions were asked of me. I was surprised to learn that Vuutey's two sons could speak a little English. One of his sons tried speaking with me, but the other son, was too shy to try. That night, I slept in my brother's home on a wooden-frame bed. They did not have a mattress, just rice mats that they offered to put on the flat wooden bedframe for me. Although I was so tired, it was difficult to fall asleep. I felt nervous about closing my eyes, with no secure doors and windows. My brother-in-law, Hey, stayed up all night, to keep a watchful eye for any prowlers during the night. I was embarrassed by his efforts to stay up all night, just to watch the property for me. Over the next few days, Vuutey arranged some of his police officers to monitor the area near his home to keep an eye on the house. As word would eventually get out that there was an American visitor, some bandits might be attracted to the area for a visit. This was not just a precaution but a very real threat.

The next morning, I got up very early, but not before many of my nieces and nephews were already up. Vuutey hired someone to go and get my sister Met, to let her know that I had returned home. When she came, she cried so much. She was so happy to see me. That morning, I opened up my giant roller-bag filled with clothes, and I showed them all the clothes that I had brought for them. They were so excited. For the rest of the time that I was there, they were all wearing the different clothes that I had brought with me. In Seattle, Seim's wife, Pah, helped me pick them out at a second-hand store the week before I left for my trip. My youngest nieces were so darling in their little dresses. The English writing was very interesting for them on the T-shirts.

My sister Pah showed me a small area in my father's hut where there were several items stowed away. I could not believe my eyes when I discovered that all of my clothes from fourteen years ago, along with personal items that I had left behind, were neatly kept, safely put away, to wait my return one day. I could not hold back my tears in amazement. The dam of locked-up memories was suddenly broken, and the memories came crashing into my mind. All of a sudden, I was a sixteen-year-old boy again, with my many plans of trading around Cambodia with my friends. With one shirt, that was one of my favorites, I saw myself on the train, traveling across Cambodia. Then with another, I saw myself sitting with my friends in the late evening at the nighttime bazaars in Phnom Penh. I saw my life as it was fifteen years ago, and I felt like I was back again to continue where I had left off. This felt like the best thing to do. I picked up my favorite shirt and tried to put it on, but I could not get it over my shoulders. It was way too small for me, as I was now really thirty and not sixteen anymore. It was all so amazing for me. If my clothes only knew where I had been while I was away. They had kept everything, despite their poverty. Everything was left untouched, just as I had left it. My father missed me over the years, as did everyone. In some small way, these belongings replaced me while I was absent. Those belongings were me. I looked through everything, so amazed. Unfortunately, none of the shirts fit me, as I was not the skinny teenager that I once was. So I offered my clothes to Vuutey, who could still fit into them, to wear. He gladly accepted them.

Later that morning, I gave the adults their gifts. I wanted to unload some of the money that I was carrying, before I somehow lost it, or had it stolen from me. To each of my sisters, and brother, I gave US$400. I also gave US$400 to my father. Met and Paht both cried when they saw the money. My sister Met, through her tears, told me that she could work for the rest of her life and would never have as much money as that. My sister Met was extremely poor, as her husband did not work often and had taken to alcohol. With their seven children, life was very desperate at times. I told her to make sure that the money was used for her and the children and not any alcohol. I did not want to preach, but I did not want them to think that I could afford to give them this kind of money all of the time. My brother, Vuutey, and his wife, Toll, were very grateful, as were my other sisters. When I saw Lye Lye, later that day, she also cried so much, that I started to cry too. It was so amazing to see her sweet face again, and to see how she had fully grown up. I also gave them different gifts that I had purchased over the past eight years in anticipation of my visit. I had brought five solid gold necklaces, each worth about US$750, which could be melted down in an emergency, if they needed to do so. In Cambodia, this is a common practice, costing only about US$2. In a country where the currency fluctuated so much, it was better to keep money in American dollars and gold. American dollars, as well as gold, were readily accepted anywhere in Cambodia.

During the day, I stayed low and sat indoors to avoid the intense heat outside. My nieces and nephews followed me around the house when I moved, readjusting the two electric fans that they had there. I stayed at either my brother's house or Pah's house during my visit. They had electricity twenty-four hours each day, whereas my other sisters only had it from 6:00 a.m. to 11:00 p.m., to save on the expense. I could not stand the heat even in the cooler nights without the fans. I was gone so long that I was no longer acclimated to the heat.

My relatives would come into the house each day to ask me many questions about America. They wanted to know everything about me, Seattle, and the American people. My father asked me how much the plane ticket cost to come back to Cambodia. I told him that the round-trip ticket, not including the round-trip flight from Phnom Penh, was US$1,400. My sister Pah gasped on hearing that. For her, it must have seemed like a million dollars. My father also wanted to know how long the trip took, so I explained about the international date line and the many hours of flying. I also explained to them the difficulty that I faced when buying a ticket to Battambang during the New Year, because so many other people were also willing to pay to travel then. Unfortunately, no one received my letters that were mailed a month before, so my visit was a complete surprise. Pah said that it was going to be an excellent year as I came at the very beginning of the New Year. It is a belief in Cambodia that God—or I should mean the Great Buddha, their closest equivalent to the western concept of God—came to all the people on New Year's Eve, bringing good luck. They had no idea who Santa Claus was, but symbolically, the idea of bringing happiness by sharing gifts among family and friends is very much like this; however, much greater spiritual meaning is involved.

On that day, my second eldest sister, Paht, told me about some very sad misfortunes that her family had suffered. She had seven children, but only four were still alive. One of her sons, four years ago, was walking only three hundred meters from the house, with a neighbor friend of the same age. One of them stepped on a landmine that was buried there some time ago. There was nothing left of either of the boys' bodies. It was very sad. Paht explained how they only heard the noise of the explosion, and "That was it!" Both boys were around seven years old, and they were just doing their chores of watching the cows—the same as I had done, at about that age, years ago along the river. There were no landmines then. Last year, her two twin daughters, of five years, died. The disease was mysterious. One of them died first, and then in a few days, the other died as well. Paht explained how she visited the *Horah*, a type of fortune teller several months before, out of desperation, and was told that her house was the source of bad luck. The *Horah* exhorted that my sister would have to tear down her home, and build again, to end the trend of bad fortune. It was the bad energy in her home that caused the death of her children. Ever since she heard this, Paht wanted to raise the money to build a new house on her property. As this fortune teller was well-respected, Paht was very anxious about her need to build a new home but could not afford to do so. I wanted to help her, and seeing that her home really needed to be replaced anyway, I empathized, but I was not sure that I could help her. My father also had a very leaky roof on his thatched hut. I knew in advance that they might need some extra help with things, but I did not anticipate them needing so much. I agreed to go ahead and pay the US$150 to have a new roof built on my dad's hut. His hut was only about 130 square feet in size, so it was a very small metal roof that I purchased for the top of his hut. Also, I agreed, toward the end of my visit, to pay for all the wood, cement, nails, and even the labor that was needed to build a new house for Paht. It only cost me about US$1,000, a great deal of money for me back in America, but nothing compared to the price of an American home. I knew that they would never have the money to do those things, and I felt it was better to be there when they spent the money, than to later wire it to them, not knowing where the money really went. She was so thankful, and my father was very proud and grateful for me. I also decided that in the near future, I would send Paht the money to buy a row boat for the flooding season. Only Pah had a boat, and Paht always had to wait, with her children, for all of Pah's family to be finished using it, before her family could utilize it. Despite the fact that both she and her husband worked every day, they were still very poor, even for Cambodian standards.

I was glad to give them money in person, instead of by wire. The family business that I had been sending money through to Cambodia had been very honest. But apparently, my father's recently divorced wife, had not been very generous with sharing the money that I was sending to my family. A good portion of the money had been used to support her own son, instead of my father, and the rest of my family. That maddened me, and I felt it was strange on the last telephone conversation that I had with my family more than a year ago, that my ex-stepmother, kept insisting on needing more money after I had just sent them US$1,000. I could not understand how they could have already spent it. Fortunately, Vuutey and Paht discovered that she had been hoarding much of the money that I was sending them, and they asked my father to divorce her, to get her away from the family. The woman was no longer living near my family. It is sad, that greed can get the most of some people. Unfortunately, she was able to take a big portion of the land that he still had left, after the government had already taken away so much. She apparently had some kind of pull with the local government, or her son did. As a result, my father's hut was actually now on the land that he had originally set aside for Paht and her family. Vuutey's present home stood on the original place, where my boyhood home had once stood. At least they still had the small portion of land near the train station, where they could make money with their restaurant and booth. I was glad to hear that my father had no more intentions of marrying. He already had two fine marriages to my natural mother, Vanna, and my stepmother, Lem.

On the second day that I was there, I gave all of the remaining knick-knacks that I brought with me to my nieces and nephews. I gave my nephew June a camera that he was very excited about. To my nieces, I gave some pearls that could be made into earrings, which I bought in Hawaii. I also gave away a bracelet that was strung together by small decorative elephants, to my eldest niece, Saphon. I also went ahead and gave all thirty-two of my nieces and nephews US$30 each. I gave US$100 for every three of them, to divide up evenly between them. One of my nieces was so cute, because she used part of the money that I gave her to buy a ring for her finger so that she would always have something to remind her of me. The rest of the money, she planned to save. June, unfortunately, was playing with some friends and set his camera down for just a moment on a bench in the city. When he looked for it, the camera was gone. Someone had already stolen it. I felt bad for him, but I would not replace it, because I had to let him know that it was very important to hold on to his possessions and to treat them carefully. He still had the other US$30 that I gave him.

One of my nephews, Chan, had fallen off a coconut tree just a couple of weeks before I was there. He tried to climb up the tree to get some fresh coconut milk, and while he was at the top, he slipped, falling all the way to the ground, breaking his leg. There were very few doctors in the area, and they were very expensive. He limped whenever he walked around our area of the village. I hoped that he would go to the doctor, but the reality was that there were very few doctors in the region. Apparently, there was still quite a shortage of doctors, as the Khmer Rouge had wiped out most of the medical community during their reign of terror. From what I understood, it might be years before many doctors would make their way to remote towns again. I insisted he go and paid for the doctor to treat him.

Saphon, Paht's eldest daughter, was also born in the Khmer Rouge village. She was also very lucky to have survived the holocaust as a baby. Her warm-heartedness and diligence were very apparent to me, while I was there. She took care of my father every day. She would work all day, assisting men in building homes with setting cement blocks in the ground, and then in the evening, she would come home and help my father with whatever he needed to have done. She washed his clothes every day and helped him to bathe too. My father was getting very old and very fragile. He had lived a very long and difficult life. I still remember him from my boyhood, as being very tall for a Cambodian, about six feet. He was also very strong. In the past several years, he had aged tremendously. His size was much smaller, and he could not really walk at all by himself. He would often sit and watch us in a calm and contemplative way, and when he spoke, everyone would listen carefully, as he often spoke so profoundly and with wisdom. His mind was still quite clear. My father talked about how glad he was that the fighting, that he had known since he was a boy, seemed to have subsided over the past six years.

Saphon always helped my father to make sure that he was comfortable while he sat. He was very lucky to have such a good and caring granddaughter as Saphon. I told Saphon to stop working her day job, and that I would send her US$300 per month to take care of my father. This was a lot of money for me back in America, but it was well worth it for me to send the money to have her take care of my father. It was next to impossible to bring any of my family to America, and it was not the easiest transition for anyone to go through too. So sending them money was the best thing that I could do to help my family. From her work each day, she made only US$100 per month—it is unbelievable to think about, as that would only cover dinner for one, at the Space Needle Restaurant in Seattle. Yet that was her earnings for the entire month. I knew that earnings were very low in Cambodia, but I had forgotten just how low, until I saw it firsthand again. But there was hope, as long as peace continued and business enterprises thrived. Maybe someday my family would be able to live much easier. For the little ones that played around the village, I hoped that they would see prosperity, as opposed to the constant war and poverty that Cambodians of my generation saw for most of their lives. I was extremely lucky that at such an early age, I had older friends who taught me how to do the trading business between cities; otherwise, I certainly never would have had the resources to go all the way to America.

My family was so amazed with my pictures of Seattle, Hawaii, and other places in the places in the Pacific Northwest. They loved the picture of my car. None of them could fathom how much the car cost me in America. American cars were never seen in that part of Cambodia, as most of the cars there were second-hand Toyotas, or new Nissan trucks. American cars were never seen, as they were untouchably expensive. In describing other features of American cities, I found it difficult to explain the concept of skyscrapers. I tried explaining how some of them reached seventy or more stories in height. One of my nephews retorted with, "How could they possibly climb up there," as he had never been on an elevator before. Most of my family had never even been to Phnom Penh. They enjoyed seeing pictures of all of my Caucasian friends, as some had never seen Caucasians before. No one in my family had a TV, and American movies were very rare and hard to come by. There were no cinemas there. My family loved posing for my camera and camcorder. Yet, occasionally I would forget the superstitions and do a faux pas without thinking. For example, I tried to get three of my relatives in a picture together. Vuutey stopped me saying, "No way. That is very bad luck. You cannot do that." I had forgotten that three people in a picture spells doom for those in the picture, a superstition that I had completely forgotten. One of my baby nephews was very shy of the camcorder, and he would begin screaming every time I took his picture, so I stopped that right away. He did not know what it was that I was doing.

Pah told me not to show anyone the video of our home and area, as she was ashamed of their poverty, so I agreed to show the video to no one other than my closest friends. My nephew Tear would always accompany me, while I was video-taping everyone. He liked hearing me describe everyone in English. Everyone laughed as I spoke English, because no one could understand what I was saying.

My different relatives kept touching my hands and face, and they liked to look at my American-style haircut. They would look at my skin and comment on how soft it was. I told them that in America, they have moisturizers for dry skin. I explained how many Americans were very conscious about their appearance, and fitness was important to many. I told them about how some Americans would go running or work out each day. They thought this idea was very odd, as they all worked very hard during the day, and for them, the idea of exercise seemed remotely foreign, or just plain ridiculous. I told them that because of the richer foods in America, a person had to exercise to prevent themselves from becoming fat. I brought vitamins to give to my father, but they did not agree with his digestion. They did for him, what coconut milk now did for me. But my uncles and aunts liked the vitamins and readily took them. I also gave aspirin and other over-the-counter remedies to my sisters and brother for their children. They appreciated them, but I did not bring any pills aside from the chewable vitamins and aspirin, for fear of someone getting a hold of them and overdosing on them by accident. I had three extra toothbrushes that I gave away to some of my nieces who wanted them.

We spent some nights discussing how my father lost almost all of his land, because the government confiscated it. Land was continually reassessed to people, as wealthy people from Hong Kong, China, Thailand, Singapore, and Vietnam would buy up premium city lots, forcing more and more tenants to live on land in the countryside. Originally, my father owned approximately thirty acres of land. Now all that he had was about a forty-meter square lot that he shared with my sister Paht. People in the government who would arrange the sale, personally profited with under-the-table commissions or bribes. It was part of the corruption that was continuing on in the government that needed to be changed, but the common people were powerless to do anything about this problem. We were all thankful that the Khmer Rouge finally surrendered the year before. Unfortunately, there were always many problems with the government.

It was quite amazing that Vuutey had gained so much status as the head of the police for Sisophon. So for bandits, or thieves, et cetera, he had some control of that problem and gave my family a strong sense of security. It was the "white collar" crime in government offices or decisions made about the direction of "land resources" that caused families to lose their land over time. After the Khmer Rouge, many areas of land were unclaimed for periods of time, as people never returned. Also, large swaths of land became interesting to developers, or to individuals seeking to acquire more land for no real purpose other than to have it. Deeds were created, and complications arose over who owned what areas. I am not fully sure how my father's land became so much smaller, and my father did not want to talk about it. He lost more of it due to the divorce from his last wife. Luckily, my brother and sisters retained several small parcels connected together, not far from the river and the nearby newer train station. Vuutey's wife kept a restaurant operating near the station out of a portion of their home to create a little income.

My Aunt Oiy and Uncle Druin were able to retain their property on the hill. On one of the days that I stayed with my brother in Sisophon, my Aunt Oiy came to visit. She was now in her mid-sixties. As her husband, my Uncle Druin, had died about four years before, she shaved her head, as was the custom for widows in Cambodia. Most of the older women in the family had shaved their heads, as most were widowed. My Aunt Oiy upon seeing me was so happy. During one of our conversations, I decided to bring up the topic of the Khmer village, and all that she did for me, in talking to the *Rem* to convince him into letting me stay in her village to work, and her sneaking food to me on that first night in her village. She smiled. I could sense that she appreciated me for bringing it up. Aunt Oiy still had many coconut trees on her land, and on one of the days, Vuutey encouraged me to drink lots of coconut milk. My Americanized digestive system produced the worst-ever diarrhea imaginable as a result. How I ever was able to drink coconut milk like water when I was a boy, I do not know. Thankfully, I had brought medication with me to protect me for just that reason.

My cousin Eep was married, with several children. She and her husband were doing all right, with their food selling business in the town's market. Aunt Oiy's son, Dune, never returned home after the war. He was one of my best friends growing up. Some people returned a few years later when they were finally released or escaped from the Khmer Rouge strongholds in the countryside. But others never did return. One of my cousins who was held as a prisoner since 1975 was finally released just a few years earlier, and she was allowed to return home. Her name was Yee, and her father had moved to Revere Beach in Boston. They assumed the worst, and they also were able to go through their own immigration story to get to America.

We shared many stories together, and shared our thanksgivings as well, to still be alive after so much had taken place in our lives. We were so incredibly lucky and fortunate to have survived so much. My father finally told me one evening, before he went to bed, that everyone in the family loves me, and that everyone will always love me, but still, it is not safe to live there with them. It is better to take advantage of the life that I had built for myself in America. My father told me how proud he was of the person that I had become. I loved my father so much. I especially loved his courage and wisdom. In his kind, loving, and softly spoken sweet words, he had granted me his forgiveness for my leaving Cambodia during my adolescent years to chase the dream I had of going to America.

My brother, Vuutey, lived fairly well—a person could do so on US$280 per month there. It was very good, compared to the quality of life that most endured in such an impoverished area. Vuutey did not take advantage of his rank, as some police chiefs in other regions did, where they would ask for money from business owners and other prosperous people in the rural areas in exchange for protection. He did not feel that this was right, and he felt that this only added to the corruption in the present government. The earnings that Vuutey and his wife made from their little restaurant allowed them to buy other items for their family, that Vuutey's salary would not cover. Their wooden house was actually the largest among the many that were in the area near the train station.

Each day, travelers who were waiting for the train, primarily merchants, would eat at their outdoor restaurant, sometimes filling up all the tables in the front of their house. Each day, the train would reach the end of the line in Sisophon Station at about 10:00 a.m. The train would then leave Sisophon for Battambang at about 2:00 p.m. So for the last hour, before the train left, many people would visit the different restaurants that were in people's homes along the tracks.

Usually, my sister-in-law just served the patrons, as their waitress, although she was an excellent cook. My brother and sister-in-law paid for another person to cook. One of the most popular dishes that people ate was *Chinangplung*, a type of shabu-shabu Cambodian style, made from mixed meats of chicken, pork, and beef with different vegetables along with mint in boiling water. The dish was served in a bowl that had a small burner underneath. Another popular dish was *Bahgong*, or giant lobster soup. *Me Cha*, the Cambodian version of *Paht Thai*, the name of the dish in the nearby Thailand, was another favorite. This was made from rice noodles, beef, bean sprouts, mint, and assorted vegetables. Curry was also popular. Chicken, lemon grass, coconut milk, and hot curry were all cooked together and served on rice. Their restaurant was popular when I was there. When they finished eating, they were able to take a nap in the front portion of the house, while waiting for the train. My sister-in-law would wake them up a few minutes before the train departed.

My family worked so hard, and for the most part, a great deal of happiness could be found in their village, despite their adversities. Just the same as when I was a child—they did not have that much, but at the same time, they had so very much. I felt so good to be back home with my family, once again reunited after so much time had passed.

16

SISOPHON, CAMBODIA

The train station still featured the name "Sirasaphon," which is the formal name for my city. It was still abbreviated to "Sisophon," which is the old name of the city, that may be as old as its neighboring city of Battambang, which has traceable history to before the tenth century. I heard the name Sirasaphon much more commonly than I used to, during my revisit, as compared to when I was growing up. Both Sisophon and Sirasaphon were still used interchangeably.

The station and my family's land was about three-fourth of a kilometer from the city center, where a central public market and bus station are located. Sirasaphon was situated on higher ground, where it did not flood, on the base of a large hill called Phnom Swai. *Phnom* means mountain in Cambodia; *Swai* means mango. On the top of Phnom Swai was a beautiful temple called Wat Phnom Swai. It had been rebuilt after the Khmer Rouge razed most of the buildings on the site. When I was a child, there was a hole in the ground on top of the Phnom Swai that opened to a large underground chamber that led to the Sisophon River, which came out of the mountain about one kilometer away. People used to drop coconuts in the hole to transport the coconuts to lower ground. My sister Pah explained to me that in the years since I had left, the hole was sealed up because it was believed that a powerful, angry ghost lived in the hole.

I do not know who decided this, but this is what had been done. There was a claim that birds could not even fly over the hole without falling inside. The area now had a playground and a large park, with a newly rebuilt temple site. When I was a child, a thousand or more steps led down the far side of the mountain to Wat Chom Gah Kanol, which was about two kilometers away from my father's home. The temple, which was named after a fruit tree, indigenous to Cambodia, known as the jackfruit tree in the West, was the temple that Vuutey and I went to see after the war, where we discovered that the reports of the body landfills were true. According to Pah, everything had been cleaned up, yet the temple was no longer as beautiful as it once was, because there was not enough money to rebuild the prominent structures that once stood there. Instead, the temple was made of thatched huts, near the ancient banyan tree that still grew there. The stairs that were destroyed were never rebuilt, but instead, a steep trail still existed. When I was a child, we sometimes stopped by Wat Chom Gah Kanol on the way to see the land that my father used to have where he grew banana trees. I did not revisit the temple on my visit.

In the years of being away, a new public building had been constructed, all in brick and sandstone, that housed the public market. Booths were rented out daily to merchants. During the time when I did my grading business, the market was in the open air. People would put mats on the ground or set up table to display various items they had for sale. Sisophon did not have a bank, nor any substantial buildings other than the public market which was about the size of two city blocks. In the city, there were three hotels and Sisophon College, just off the city market. For two of the days that I was there, I decided to stay in the air-conditioned International Hotel. The hotel had the same name as the one I had stayed at in Battambang city. It was comfortable enough, and they charged me just US$10 per night. There was a brand new hotel that was closer to my family's home, but it only had a large ceiling fan in the rooms, and no air-conditioning. Among other changes in the city, many of the homes now featured store fronts on the first floor. Businesses were more common.

The city was still covered with small wats. These neighborhood places of worship were ubiquitous. The small wat located within about one hundred meters from my father's home was Wat Luc Yun—the meaning is the Vietnamese Temple. This temple was very small and run down but still modestly maintained. The small wat was very old, as it had been there when my father was a boy, and most likely when my father's father was also a boy. There were many smaller wats throughout Cambodia's countryside that were in disrepair, as there was not enough money to repair them all. The road along Highway 5 traveled just below Wat Phnom Swai, on its way toward Poipet and Thailand. Highway 5 connected to Highway 6, not far from my home, which passed by Wat Swai on the way toward Angkor Wat, about a hundred kilometers away. Sisophon is about midway between Battambang and Angkor Wat.

The provincial name for the region had changed, as more and more people moved to the thriving region since I had left. Rice production was the primary source of industry in the region, and although the Khmer Rouge still had outposts in the northwestern part of Cambodia, until very recently, the population continued to prosper, compared to other regions in Cambodia. The city of Sisophon was growing and is now part of the province of Bantheay Meanchey, no longer the province of Battambang, as when I had left.

Yet Sisophon was still the sleepy town that it was when I lived there, with the slight hustle in the city center where the merchants did all kinds of trading each day. There was also a smaller market just outside the city that used to be a military training camp during the Lon Nol years, just prior to the Khmer Rouge takeover. Lon Nol was an American-supported prime minister. This smaller market, which I used to frequent during my trading days, had a curiosity for me, so I decided to go there one day during my visit home to see how things had changed. There were about the same number of people trading there as in the days that I was there. Two people in the market recognized me, and they were so surprised to see me, asking me where I had been for so long. I told them that I have been living in America. They could not believe it, as they never expected that of me, or of anyone that they knew for that matter, to make it all the way to America. That was a strange feeling.

The landmines along the Sisophon tributary were supposedly all cleaned up, but I would not go with my family down along the river to swim. I did not want to risk it. My interest in adventure had diminished substantially over the years, especially as I had so much of it during my youth. I had friends back in America that would have been angry with me, if I had been so foolhardy as well. It was one of my dreams for Cambodia, that all of the landmines that had been scattered throughout the country would one day be entirely cleaned up.

I was surprised by the number of new Nissan trucks that drove through the streets of the city. Many of the residents used their trucks in the trade between the cities of Aranyaprathet, Poipet, Battambang, and Sisophon, and they were prospering well enough with the trade, that they were able to afford brand new vehicles. Nissan and Hyundai seemed to be the most popular brand of vehicle in the town. Small color TVs were fairly common in people's homes. While walking around the city, I could hear them from the outside through their open windows. My nephews and nieces kept begging me to take them to the movies. I asked them where the movie theater was, and they told me that it was at a neighbor's house, on their thirteen-inch TV set. The neighbor down the street charged one thousand riels, the equivalent to twenty-five American cents per person to watch the movie on their TV. I felt kind of annoyed with the neighbors, but I guess, it was a type of business for them, as TVs were still a commodity, so to speak. They never had access to American movies, as they were way too expensive. They were only able to see Chinese or Thai movies. I teased them, saying how an American movie theater was something much different. I bought a TV for them before I left. I also bought a wheelchair for my father, so my family could take him around the village near his home much more easily.

17

FORGOTTEN MEMORIES

After being back in my hometown, even earlier memories returned to me, from the age of two or three that I had long since forgotten. They may have been triggered by my visit back home, by the contrasts of now being an American and of being a Cambodian back then. In the years before the Khmer Rouge, there was the Vietnam War, and all that went along with that. On the side of Cambodia, war was raging between a wide variety of forces. King Sihanouk of Cambodia had an unclear position, as the Vietnam War began to spread over to Cambodian soil. Our hero king who gained independence for Cambodia from the French, just twenty years before, was losing popularity as a result. The Vietcong were residing in villages within Cambodia. At first, it was Sihanouk who agreed to let the Americans fly over Cambodia to bomb the potential villages, where the Vietnamese communists were supposedly hiding. Sihanouk later changed his mind, after siding with the other power center, China, and the other communist movement that were fighting in the region, after he was deposed by General Lon Nol. During the Vietnam War, the fighting frequently spilled over on to Cambodian territory, near Svay Rieng and Prey Veng, along the Vietnam and Cambodian border, The American B-52 bombings were becoming more common. Sisophon and

Battambang, on the other side of Cambodia, were never bombed; however, the B-52s during some missions would fly overhead in so many numbers, from the direction of Thailand, that the ground shook, as if it were an earthquake or something like that. Although I was so little, I can still remember the B-52s. In Cambodian, the "B" pronounced with the French accent sound like "beh." And in the Cambodian number system, fifty-two is pronounced "hap be," so you would hear people yelling the phrase "beh hap be." Over and over. It was years later, after learning English, that "beh hap be" and the phrase "be happy" had such great irony, as they sound so much alike; however, the meaning behind them both were so much different. The B-52s flying overhead meant sheer terror for the villagers. As soon as time allowed, after the rainy season each year, my family would dig a deep trench for hiding. When the B-52s were spotted or heard, my family would hide there. When they flew over our home during the floods, there was nothing we could do except stay in our homes, hoping that bombs would not be dropped. Every time the planes would fly overhead, there was screaming and pandemonium, as my sisters, brother, and I were all rounded up and taken to the trench with our mother, uncle, and father, or whoever happened to be around, at the time of the raid.

During the two years prior to the Khmer Rouge takeover, as rumors spread about the heavy bombing of the countryside, the sight of the planes caused intense fear. We never knew if they would eventually bomb our village or not. Each year as the flood waters rose, the trenches would wash out, filling up with new debris from the river, so each year new trenches had to be made. Years later, when I was doing my trading business, I would still see the remains of some of the trenches and craters left from bombs along the railroad tracks, especially in the area between Kampong Chhnang and Phnom Penh in the countryside. These shelters were useful in protecting families from shrapnel and flying debris, yet if a bomb was dropped inside the trench, it was all over for the family inside. The B-52s never dropped their bombs on my father's land, as the fighting was fairly exclusive to the far side of Cambodia. However, as the Khmer Rouge infiltrated Battambang, the carpet raids were getting nearer and nearer, especially in 1973, right before the end of the Vietnam War. In the areas that never succumbed to the annual flooding, trenches and huge craters remained for years as a testament to those very strange frightening times. Also, the area along the railroad tracks were the most noticeably bombed, as the tracks were often targeted in the raids. Although the United States had not officially declared war on Cambodia, twice the tonnage of bombs was dropped on the Cambodian countryside during the Vietnam War than on Japan during WWII.[4]

Other memories came back to me from the period of one to two years prior to Lon Nol losing power to the Khmer Rouge, when I was about seven or eight years old. Around the clock, as the different forces fought through-out all of Cambodia, gunfire was constantly heard. Once America pulled out of Vietnam, Lon Nol was faced with a losing battle. And it was not too long after the fall of Saigon that Lon Nol's troops were finally defeated. Yet, with a great deal of luck, fighting did not occur within the city of Sisophon or Battambang, at least none that I was aware of at that time. My father used to tell me stories that he had heard of the Khmer Rouge taking over villages and making the villagers fight along with them against their will. If they chose not to go along, they and their entire family would be killed. One story that scared me terribly was one of how the Khmer Rouge would sometimes tie bombs around the body of a villager and send them off to the neighboring village where the Lon Nol forces were stationed. The boy or youth would be told that if he returned to his own village, his family would be executed. Most of the time, the youths would be caught in the woods by Lon Nol's soldiers before them ever entering the neighboring villages. They were usually shot, or who knows what else, as the bombs could go off at any time. I was so scared, being a boy of eight, when my father told me that story. I was so afraid that our small village, in the suburbs of Sisophon, would be captured and that I would be forced to do the same.

I discussed some of these memories with my father on my visit. My earliest memory of America was of a country of vast fire power, with the

4 Steinberg, *In Search of Southeast Asia*, p. 379.

most powerful bomb; I assumed, during my boyhood, that it was the power to blow up a giant house. I did not learn about the A-bomb until after living in America for a couple of years. After General Lon Nol, the pro-American general, took over Cambodia in the spring of 1970, while King Sihanouk was abroad in Paris, Americans were not thought of as an enemy because they always dropped food supplies to Lon Nol's troops when they were occupied fighting against the Vietnamese communists or the Khmer Rouge. However, the Cambodian people did not appreciate the American bombing raids in the least as many thousands of Cambodians were killed as a result. When Lon Nol's regimen fell, and Pol Pot's Khmer Rouge seized control in 1975, we were instructed to hate Americans. It was all so confusing when I was growing up, as I could never understand fully who was on what side and what side stood for what cause. There were bombs, powerful planes, sounds of gunfire in the distance, and reports of war everywhere, as well as the frightening stories in my boyhood. There was also the forced labor camps of the Khmer Rouge; why was life so difficult? We were also taught while growing up that China was the richest country in the world. France was not far behind them in wealth, as I understood it then. In the small city of Sisophon, all we knew was that the B-52s were very scary and posed imminent danger, although they never bombed us.

In fact, no one could really figure out who the true enemy was. There were many. We just did what we were told, but one thing was certain, which was that we all hated the Khmer Rouge, Although April 17 marks the day that the infamous Khmer Rouge took over, it is still celebrated as both a memorial to the holocaust and for its official name, "The Victory over American Imperialism Day." After being gone so long from my country, I did not know this until recently, as I only knew it as a day of scorn for the Khmer Rouge. I had only lived in Cambodia for a few years following the emancipation from the Khmer Rouge by the Vietnamese communists. So I can understand the political reality behind this official holiday.

The horrors and atrocities that I witnessed during my early years flooded back into my mind during both my waking hours and heavy dreaming. My life has not been an easy one, and I hoped that since I have survived so much, I will live a very long life in good health back in America. Of course, my life could always come to a quick halt at any time. Yet, to have lived through so much already, I am very thankful. I am also grateful for those friends and family members who have helped me along the way. In America, very few people could even guess my story—so complicated that for some, it is too troublesome to even mention, and for others, it must seem like a hundred years long, not just thirty. In America, the general public was not made aware of the bombing raids in Cambodia until much later, as the original evidence was shredded.[5] I believe that I had some special spirits protecting me, or helping me along the way, to get through all that I had witnessed. I still think about my mother, whom I lost while I was so young. My life was actually quite pleasant during my first few years, until the terror of the evacuation under the Khmer Rouge. I did not visit the gravesite of my stepmother, Lem, as my time was so short back home. I intended to in the future. So many memories flooded my mind with emotions of all kinds, as I reflected on so many people that I encountered during the many trying times that I have faced.

I was also so happy and grateful to be with my family again. I felt truly whole for the first time in fourteen years. There had been so much pain, and loneliness at times, especially in the camp in Thailand, and in the first two years of resettling in America, that sometimes, I wondered what it was all meant to be about. I was so lucky that so many in my family were still alive. To feel their loving embraces, pats on the back, and smiling faces again, I felt as if I were in heaven. If there was anything to be derived from all the evil and good that I had encountered on the way, it was to share in the love and joy of my family and closest friends. I cannot be mad about my struggles and the innumerable injustices that I experienced. There is not enough time, even if I were to live for another thousand years.

There is no suitable punishment that I am aware of that fully fits the crimes that the Khmer Rouge committed. A person cannot be brought back from the final sentence of death. A price could never fully be paid to make

5 Shawcross, Sideshow. Nixon, Kissenger, and the Destruction of Cambodia, p. 350.

up for the years of separation from family. Abuses, tortures, and maimings cannot be turned around. Tears shed cannot be completely forgotten. One of the most sensible and positive phrases that I have come across concerning the loss of loved ones and enduring great evil was the following phrase that I heard: "Only through love, can someone move forward. Hate destroys everything." This statement was made on a televised news broadcast, by an African American woman concerning her lost loved ones in the Oklahoma city bombing. She summed it up so eloquently, the way that I had long since decided to cope in life. I have tried my best to turn the pain of separation from my family into good. I have also done all that I could in my life to put the evil that I experienced in the camps behind me. I did care, but if I cared too much, I would go crazy if I did not try to let it all go. I just focused on the present and the love that was around me in the present moment. Forgiveness is also so important, but difficult to fully embrace, as there is so much to remember to forgive.

Sometimes, in the village, I wondered if we would all disappear from the world without a trace, without anyone ever knowing about us, about our way of life, or about the evil events that transpired for us. In the many times when I felt that I was not meant to live a long life, I always believed that my own soul would somehow be protected from the evil all around me, although my temporal existence may end up being quite short and meaningless in itself. But I did not focus on this, as my strongest motivation to stay alive sprang not from fear but from my deep desire to see my whole family again, all reunited back in Sisophon. I was filled with anger so much of the time, but there was nothing that I could do out of fear of what might happen to me if I spoke or lashed out. I felt very angry for being forced to leave my comfortable, happy life behind in Sisophon. I hated the Khmer Rouge for the separation from my brother and elder sisters, and from having to leave my animals behind on the farm. I wanted to crush the Khmer Rouge like squishing an egg. I visualized this over and over again in my mind. The Khmer Rouge killed good people, and they did not care. For me, the Khmer Rouge were pure evil, and they were the worst people imaginable and I no longer viewed them as even being human. My father explained to me how some people are born with the evil blood, and during their lifetimes, they lust for killing people and hurting others. If they cannot overcome their "evil blood" or bad Karma, then at the end of their life, their soul is not reborn, and they do not enter nirvana either—their soul is destroyed and its energy dispersed, like dust in the wind. None of us know, but we all know in our heart of hearts, when we are around individuals of high caliber, honesty, integrity, and high ideals, you can almost sense the change in a room.

I just focused on working hard and trying to stay low in the camp, out of the minds of the soldiers. I worked so hard, to save myself time and time again. I was more fortunate than many, to still have my wise, intelligent father, and brave stepmother, to help me through the most difficult times. It was the love of my family that made me want to live. Many people "cracked" after experiencing so much trauma. Some people suffered severe amnesia and could not remember anything that happened to them. Other people went crazy after their loved ones were killed. Deep down, my cornerstone of sanity that helped me to be strong was my own fundamental sense that each person's soul would receive its just rewards. At the time, I could not put it into words, but I just had an acceptance of this being the way things were. In my Buddhist upbringing, I believe that if warmth and love emanated from one's soul, then warmth and love emanated back toward it. If evil, pain, and hate emanated from one's soul, then evil, hate, and pain emanated back toward it. People can laugh at this scheme after doing great evil, but their laugh is just a hook to pull people toward their own messy Karma, so to speak. In the afterlife, this may be enacted out in ways far beyond our human mind's capability to imagine, and in the case of the Khmer Rouge soldiers, hopefully so. My father told me that when it came to Karma, good people will eventually go onto heaven to await being reborn; they then continue their cycle of rebirths until they reach a high level of perfection in their spirit and soul, over hundreds or even thousands of lifetimes, and then they move in to a place called nirvana, a place of no rebirths but in eternal bliss and peace. Truly evil people, after they die, are not reborn, and their souls are destroyed, no longer a part of the universe. This was the part of the Buddhist philosophy that was ingrained into my mind by my father and some of the priests at Wat Swai, at an early age.

As I was a young boy, all of that made me feel a little better, yet, I was filled with so much hate and anger at times, that I just wanted to see the Khmer Rouge soldiers dead. If they were dead, I could go free to see my family again and have food to eat. I hoped that all of the Khmer Rouge solders would die, so the Cambodian people could go free. But this was not the way for me, and I was powerless to do anything. On one end, I was filled with hatred and anger, and on the other, I was filled with love and hope— together these feelings created an energizing force for me that sustained me when there was no food to eat.

Once the war ended, and I was reunited with many in my family again, I began to relearn what happiness was all about, and since then, I have always strived to be happy and to enjoy the things that I liked doing in my life. Sometimes, just being alive, being able to "just be," was the most wonderful thing in itself. I began to cherish even the little things. I was glad to see people smile again, and to have good food to eat. Just to be alive is a gift to be cherished— to be able to breathe in and out, and to smell the air. After seeing so much evil and injustice, I could only want to do good and be full of love. I wanted to live in a good place, where people could love each other and be happy and not be filled with hate and the desire to kill. I have seen too much horror in my life, terrible things, that I have come to accept as possible in humanity. In America, it seemed possible for me to build better opportunities for myself, with the help of friends, and with working extra hard to better my situation. Since somehow escaping the Cambodian holocaust, I have always disliked violence in any form. I have not understood why people would want to live this way, to create a place of bad emotions for themselves. I have not cared for it even on television or in movies. So much in my life seemed to go back to the well-put theme: "Through love, I can go forward. But in hate, I lose everything." It is a simplistic theme, yet it can be useful as a guide. I certainly have not been perfect, and my mind wanders back from time to time. Instead,

I have tried to focus on the good things in my life: my family in Cambodia, my adopted Cambodian family in America, my friends, and the things that I love to do. I am lucky to be alive, and life is a great gift to be cherished.

18

THE NEW RELIGION, BUT NOT SO NEW

Other new developments in my hometown were that Christian churches had sprung up. There were three churches now in Sisophon. St Joseph's, a Catholic church, was built only one hundred meters from my father's hut. During the Sunday service, about fifty people were inside. As an alternative to the tradition of Buddhism, more and more people were willing to look to Christianity. The conservative Buddhist traditions and philosophy were ingrained in Cambodian culture, with a long history of meditation, self-abnegation, and service to others. I was surprised to see these churches, yet some people moved away from the traditional religion to new ways of understanding their spirituality. Maybe it was reactionary, in an attempt to find the Western strength in themselves, or to find a new way of protection that Buddhism has not offered them. For the most part, the mystique of Hinduism and Buddhism was the prevailing religion in Cambodia, since its early days of grandeur, the day of Angkor Wat, almost one thousand years ago. Maybe it was a way to learn new ways from the West, in an attempt for personal betterment. In any case, I am glad that they had the freedom to choose whatever religion they wanted to follow. I have met good Christians and good Buddhists in my lifetime. There are positive aspects to both religions, as well as the negatives, that I feel to be true for myself. My only concern about the church being developed next door to my father is that it must foster peaceful, contemplative, and open-minded people. Cambodia does not need any new warring factions, but it certainly has the need for charitable, warm, and friendly administrations from any organization. I saw the development of the church in my hometown in a neutral way; however, on seeing the church not far from my father's home, I was reminded again of my boyhood times with the Buddhist monks at Wat Swai.

My father was still a devout Buddhist. As he could not walk anymore, he could no longer frequent the temple, which was just down the road from his hut, to meditate, unless Saphon, one of his many granddaughters, walked him. While revisiting my family, I did not go to the temple of my boyhood. I have some good memories of the temple with my father and mother, but in all honestly, I disliked the teachers that I had there. I was sent to the temple to learn and write Sanskrit at about the age of six. The teachers at the temple were very strict. The closest relation to this type of school in the West were the very strict Catholic schools of many years ago, with the disciplinarian nuns, as I understand them to have been. I liked some of the monks, yet I found my teacher to be a brute, who had very little patience for children's inattentiveness. As a result, my father's favorite temple did not hold the same meaning for me. Wat Swai became a place of unpleasantness. I could never please my teacher, as I was always forgetting the prayers and getting into all kinds of trouble for ridiculous things. Every day, I received harsh punishments, and I was often spanked with a bamboo stick for the slightest infraction. To make matters worse, the oppressed older boys in the temple would slap me around and kick me in the butt, as part of their daily ritual, as well. For me, it was nothing as nightmarish as the Khmer Rouge–controlled village life by any means, but I dreaded the times that I had to attend school there. My father never disciplined me even half as severely as those monks did, and I missed my mother too, who was not there to protect me. All I wanted to do was stay home and play with my brother and sisters. In retrospect, my family times of listening to my father and playing with my siblings during my early years on the family farm, did far more for my character development than the rigorous programs of prayer at the temple.

One day, I refused to go back to the temple to the mean teachers there. I showed Pah and Vuutey the bruises that I had on my legs and back from the beatings that I received from my teacher. I was too ashamed to show my father. I was often late, as the two-kilometer walk to school was long, and I had no desire to go to school there anyway, so I could not make myself walk faster. Vuutey and Pah talked to my father, and my father became very upset about the treatment that I was receiving from the monks. He could not let me return to school there after he saw the bruises, so he enrolled me into a public school nearby, and I never had to go back to the teachers at Wat Swai. The new school that I was sent to was a much happier place for me, as there were less bullies to contend with, and we didn't have to do all of the boring, rigorous prayers. I also had no more bruises, except for the occasional bruise I received doing work on the family farm. My father's decision to remove me from the Buddhist temple was one of the early events that made me respect my father even more.

Since Vuutey, at eighteen years of age, had already completed a year of living in the temple, training to become a monk, I received more lenient treatment from my father in this matter. It is hoped that there will be at least one son in the family who will spend time training to become a monk. Once that obligation is fulfilled, then the parents are protected in the afterlife. In a way, it is supposed to clear away the bad Karma in the family. My father, despite being the devout Buddhist that he was, was open minded enough to let me go to the public school instead. If the situation had been reversed, and if I were the eldest son, my father would not have been so lenient. The temple school was not free but was considered much more prestigious for studying. At least, my father did not have to pay for my schooling anymore as the public school was free.

I think that I still have a good heart anyway, despite not going through all of the rigorous training at Wat Swai. I was obviously never meant to become a monk. Being the youngest son, I had it a lot easier growing up than Vuutey, and I was actually a little spoiled. I admired my father for his liberal attitudes about the temple education. He did not see the knit-pickiness of the Buddhist school as necessary for me in having a good heart and in finding happiness in my life. Vuutey had fulfilled the family obligation when he entered the monastery for one year immediately after the death of my mother. As the Buddhist schools were more prestigious, my father did regret my stubbornness in not returning. Actually, I felt that the Buddhist school, with all of the mean, older kids, and vicious disciplinarians, was no place to learn about having a good heart and happiness. It has taken me years of living in America to learn that teachers are not all crazy and mean, like the ones that I had, during my few years of early formal education—for example, Elizabeth, at the UNHCR at the Khao I Dang refugee camp, in Thailand. I only attended the public school for a couple of years, until I was eight years of age, before the Khmer Rouge took over, abolishing schools altogether. Pol Pot, the horrible dictator was actually a school teacher originally, which made me leery of teachers who were off kilter in their viewpoints, or too extreme in their opinions, one way or another. Kindness was what I resonated with, not strict coldness.

I did not visit any of the temples in my hometown, during my revisit. In fact, I hardly ever thought about them after leaving Cambodia years ago, except on those occasions when I became very lonely. During the New Year's celebrations while growing up, I often went to Chom Gah Kanol, that was so incredibly beautiful during the festivities. My happiness came from my family. Everything else took a big second to that. I also did not go inside the new Christian church that was so close to my father's home now. I never really felt as if I could fit in there as well; however, in America, I have met some wonderful Christian people. I have always enjoyed people who operated from a loving center, no matter what religion they were from. I have not bought into the conservative, narrow views, on either side of the Pacific; however, I do agree with many of the more liberal, open-minded views of both religions. Condemning people for not choosing the beliefs, customs, or rituals of a particular religion is against my way of living. It is so unfortunate that so many buy into that kind of hate around the world.

Some of the features that I really do admire among some Christian people is their desire to reach out to do community service. It does so much for everyone, when someone offers to do something for free, on occasion, and to also not always seek the utmost retribution when accidents happen. Life is challenging, and it is wonderful when someone comes along and gives another a helping hand, and just says, "Someday help someone else out, when you can." In Buddhism, my favorite person in the temple is the *donchee, or yehgee* who can be seen only wearing white robes. *Yeh* means grandmother in Cambodian. The *yehgee* are sweet grandmotherly monks or priests of the temples. Young women are never allowed to become *yehgee*, as this would pose a problem for the chaste monks. The role of the *yehgee* was somewhat different from the male monks. The *yehgee* often did the cooking for the monks and priests, but they continued the same disciplined traditions and contemplative life of the monks and priests. I liked them the best, because they often came around the village to help with the old and sick. Sometimes they would help at funerals and comfort families when it was needed. They were the sweetest. All monks, priests, and *yehgee* can always be distinguished with their shaved heads and orange and white garments, called s*abong.* The *yehgee* only wore white and can be seen meditating while standing or sitting on the temple grounds, if they are not working. They are known for abstaining from food, except for their one meal per day. They never wore make-up or any fashionable clothing. They were, for the most part, a very peaceful group, except for the strange examples of teachers that I had at Wat Swai. It was the only place where I experienced such strict rules, aside from the Khmer Rouge. I have not had the opportunity to be that familiar with the loving, friendly nuns or priests in Christianity, other than my brief encounters with them. All I know is that they would have to be very liberal to accept me.

Aside from organized religion, I just focus on my own spirituality as building positive Karma, building a better future in this life, and possibly the next. It may be that there isn't a heaven or nirvana at the end of a single life, but only after a series of well-perfected lives. I believe that Karma is a continual flow where we are continually begetting from what we have just done a moment before, which is different from the Judgement Day concept of Christianity, and the Great Forgiveness. I strongly believe that one can have a strong influence on their life by the kind of deeds they do on a regular basis, or the big deeds that they do to help or hinder. Positive karmic events are more likely to happen when good goes before it. When I thought of how I had helped the Vietnamese soldier escape on the ship, years ago, on a business trip over the Tonle Sap, I later believed that my act of helping him, so that he could go back to see his family in Vietnam, was one of the significant events that shaped the positive chances for me of eventually reaching America.

No one deserved to die in the holocaust. I was not considered a "good boy" back at Wat Swai, although I do not really believe that I did anything truly bad. Yet, my own perspective led me to believe that in the face of extreme evil, the odds against survival can become too great. I was one of the lucky survivors, as were many in my family. I really was not sure I would survive when I worked away in the fields, starving each day, in the heat of the sun. It is my belief and hope that all those who perished have been, or will be, reborn in happier circumstances, and they are able to renew their loving bonds with their old family, in new families. Or for many, maybe they can pass on to that heavenly place of nirvana and escape any additional suffering. Yet for me, life can be a very enjoyable experience, and it is such a shame that so many people had their lives taken away from them. I have no idea why some people lived, and why others died. I also do not know why the Cambodian people have been faced with so much suffering. During the forced evacuation out of Sisophon, no one could have guessed as to how horrible and tragic life would become in the years to follow. Since I was allowed to live, maybe some important reason or explanation awaits me, that might justify my survival. I came out of the experience fairly unscathed compared to many, and this has been a source of wonder for me. I have not gone on to become a famous person or one of the "greats" in history. So my survival is a complete mystery, and I am thankful.

I cannot understand how these things are determined; the conundrum is too big for my mind. Maybe there was no reason, and I somehow survived as a result of a great deal of luck and a strong desire to live. I have also been very lucky to be able to build a happy, fun-loving life for myself in America. I truly believe that with all the challenges in life, luck and the desire to work hard for what one wants, go hand-in-hand when it comes to achievement. I just cannot understand how some people were smudged out, and how I was one of the people "chosen" to survive, after going through so much, and that I also survived through my attempt to cross the border, and in Khao I Dang for nearly six years, waiting in the refugee camp. I am also grateful for my friends whom I was able to connect with in America.

In much the same way, I cannot understand how it is determined where people will be born, whether it be America, Canada, Australia, or Zimbabwe. Why are some people born with every advantage and others born with none? Is this predestined before we are ever born? Or is everything dictated by chance? In the case of my mother, I wondered why she was the one to die from the rabid dog bite, and not someone else. Why was it my mother, who was so wonderful and loving? Maybe in some way, she was being protected from the horrors that were soon to come. Maybe, had she lived, she might have experienced even a more horrific death, and even greater pain later. Was her work here already complete? My father told me after her death that before she was born, it was decided how long she would live, and then when it was her time, there was nothing that could stop it: predetermination. This is a type of Buddhist philosophy as well, and only under extreme circumstances is this altered. For in true Buddhism, there are no accidents. Everything has some meaning, whether it be remote or obvious. For a true Buddhist, every event fits into a karmic puzzle. I certainly could not fathom that I had any choice in the matter, as the Cambodian conundrum or puzzle was not one that I would have wanted to play, yet I love my family and my heritage.

As for myself, I feel that I have been extremely lucky to have survived the Khmer Rouge years and the refugee camp in Thailand. I met a psychic in Seattle who looked at me, after being introduced to her by a friend, and she laughed, and in bewilderment, said, "without a doubt, that I was a miracle." She later called me out in an audience that I attended, surprised that she would even remember who I was. I felt she was authentic as she could not even guess as to what I had been through in my life just by looking at me. I look like a typical Southeast Asian guy, with an accent nonetheless, as my pronunciation of many English words is not exact. I have also been extremely fortunate to be accepted by the INS to immigrate to America. I feel very thankful to now live in a free country, with no war-like fighting, and with opportunities to make a better life for myself. As I know how bad things can truly become, I cherish my life in America, and I hope that my happy existence continues far into the future. I have also felt very fortunate that many in my family survived, and that I am able to send money back to them from time to time. I believe that good Karma tips the scale in favor of luck, and it can help one to overcome horrific events, but it can do nothing in the event of extreme adversity or great evil.

My family is the most important thing to me. I was so happy to see my father again, after fourteen long years. So many memories flooded my mind, of my adolescent years, and of all I persevered to do to get where I am today. I know that I caused a lot of pain when I decided to leave on my own to go to America. My family missed me so much. I hoped that I was able to remedy some of the pain that I caused, and that there could be understanding as to why I left my family behind. I felt a renewed surge of love from my family, and a renewed connection to my roots. I was accepted by my own family, despite all of my faults. They just loved me so much, as I wanted to show them how much I loved them in the best way that I knew possible. This reunion was what I longed for over the past many years. I was grateful that I was given the opportunity. My roots are Buddhist and Cambodian, although now I have grown into a new person with wider and greater perspectives in a new country.

The last gift I gave to my family, I gave to my father. It is traditional in Cambodia and also in Thailand, among some other neighboring countries, for a family to have a spirit house on the corner of their property. In this house, some of which are small, and others quite fantastically large, the ashes of their ancestors are kept. The house is a dwelling place for their ancestors' spirits, so when they return, they will not inhabit the main dwellings on the property, causing problems for the family living there. The earlier spirit house that my family had, that contained the ashes of my mother and other ancestors, was destroyed by the Khmer Rouge. I decided to purchase a huge cement spirit house, about two meter cube in size. It was a replication of the Grand Palace in Phnom Penh and very ornate. It took four people to move it from a truck to the corner of my father's property. It was a gift for my father, so that one day, when his time of passing comes, his ashes would be put in an urn and placed within a window in the large spirit house, to be displayed. The coverings to the windows are made from glass, so that future generations will know that it is their great-grandfather in there, a very honorable man, who did so much for his family.

My stay seemed to move along all too quickly. And before long, it was the morning of the day of my departure. It was a very sad day. My nephew, Tear, video-taped me as my father gave me his traditional blessing for my journey back to America. And I promised everyone that I would not forget them, and that I would come back to visit as soon as I could. On the last day, my brother and sisters accompanied me as I went by taxi back to Battambang. Twelve of my nieces and nephews went by train the day before, with Lye Lye. I checked into the International Hotel again, and we all spent the day at Lye Lye's apartment in the city. It was very small, one-story brick apartment, that she had purchased two years ago for about US$400. The walls were cracked, the paint was chipped, and the cement floors were very uncomfortable, yet it was alright for her, as that was what people in the city were accustomed to living in. However, she made it as cozy a place as she could. That night, everyone slept in my hotel room with me. The next day, everyone came to the airport with me to see me off. Everyone was crying and telling me of how they were going to miss me. I cried too, as it was one of the most difficult things I ever had to do—to board that plane for my return flight to Phnom Penh. I waved goodbye to them, trying to hold back tears as I entered the jetway.

19

PHNOM PENH, CAMBODIA

The plane traveled to Siem Reap first from Battambang Airport, before heading to Phnom Penh. I could not see Angkor Wat from the plane, as I was hoping. I decided in Battambang not to visit Angkor during this trip, which is close to Siem Reap, as I wanted to spend the most time with my family, and there was not an easy way for my father to travel there with us. Only when I was a boy, too young to remember, had I been there with my mother. I hoped that someday I would be able to revisit the ancient temple, and possibly, with some American friends.

During the flight back to Phnom Penh, I reminisced about my many shared experiences with my family. My heart had a renewed energy, and I felt a solid sense of peace for the first time in years. I was so glad to have made it back to Sisophon after having lived through so much. Years of guilt and shame had been swept away, as mounting fears and growing misunderstandings that deepened with distance dissipated now. The country had been indifferent to the levels of turmoil since I left. I was lucky to get all the way back to Sisophon, during this window of opportunity, to give them all that I could, and to be able to share with them so many of my experiences. For so many years, the Khmer Rouge remained active in the northwest corner of Cambodia, making the trip back to my hometown too tenuous for me to attempt. The Khmer Rouge had surrendered in the last year, except for a small group of rebel Pol Pot followers, which did not pose a big threat at the time. But turmoil was brewing again in Cambodia, and as the current news events were indicating, the two ruling factions of the country were at divisive odds with one another. The two elected prime ministers were vying for power (Cambodia is the only country in the world to have two concurrent prime ministers, as a result of the 1993 elections sponsored by the United Nations). Tensions were building, and it seemed as if a new civil war was imminent. There was tension even among the passengers on the plane, that I could sense. The Khmer Rouge had pretty much all surrendered; however, there was still a stronghold of soldiers that existed in the jungle at the Anleng Veng Camp. It was uncertain as to how the Khmer Rouge would play a role in the struggle—hopefully none.

I decided to stop thinking about such topics, as I had no control over them. It only made me anxious. If things began to get worse while I was still in the country, I would do all that I could to move up my departure date to get back to Seattle. I knew that in the worse-case scenario, I had friends back in America who would do all that they could to help me. A couple of my friends had offered to wire me money if I ran into trouble. I also had the number and address of the US Embassy in Phnom Penh. Tha In also told me about the Bank of Hong Kong, that could give me money from my visa card, in the wake of an emergency. Actually, I decided that it would probably be a good idea to stop by the bank to withdraw some money from my card, just as a precautionary measure. I felt that I had better keep a cushion of cash available, just in case. I had given everything I had to my family that I had carried with me. But hopefully, nothing would happen.

My mind, after thinking through my plans, wandered off to more pleasant thoughts about my previous visit to Phnom Penh, in the week before, while waiting for my flight down to Battambang. I was luckily able to relocate my old pal, Succun, who was the one with whom I did most of my trading business during my teen years. I was not able to locate any others in the short time I had there. When I found Succun, I was sure that I seemed tense and tired after the long flight, as my primary intention was to await my flight to return to Sisophon to see my family. He was so surprised and happy to see me, as we were best friends during my trading business days. While looking out at the rice paddy fields far below from the airplane, I began to reflect on my earlier visit with Succun and his family.

When I knocked on his mother's door, and Succun's younger brother opened the door, his eyes opened wide with surprise as he recognized me. Chang yelled out, "Tha's here." Everyone came to see what all the noise was about, and his mother warmly greeted me and invited me into her home. She offered me tea and pointed their electric fan in their living room toward me. She was very surprised to see me, as was everyone else. She said that she had heard that I was still stuck in Thailand and asked me where I have been, during the past several years. I explained to her that I had been living in America for the past nine years. She was shocked. She told me that several of my old customers still asked about me at the old Olympic Market. Succun's mother explained to me that Succun no longer lived there, and that he had his own house and his own family now. They offered to take me to see him. I decided to visit Succun the next day because the heat outside was already too intense. I was invited to stay and visit for dinner, which I gladly accepted. The next day, I returned to meet with Chang, and together ,we went to his brother's home on his Suzuki Viva motorcycle through the city.

As it was still the morning when we rode through the city on his motorcycle, the heat had not reached its intensity yet. Chang was an excellent driver, weaving in and out, around cars, bicyclists, cycles, and pedestrians. The dusty, warm morning breeze blew by us, as we traveled the twenty-five-minute route to Succun's home. Chang occasionally had to negotiate his way around cars and occasionally a bus or large truck, driving down the wrong side of the street. Some of the streets were narrow, where barely two cars could fit in. The main avenues were wide and spacious. In Cambodia, although some traffic rules had developed, there was still very little enforcement. Along the drive, we would also get a strong whiff of the garbage and open sewers on some of the dirtier side streets. The contrasts between the buildings were interesting, as some were quite old and run down, whereas others were quite modern, built-up into various sized complexes. On one street, I was very surprised to see a Lucky Grocery Store that looked very much like an Albertsons, or Safeway, that I had become accustomed to in America. Chang said that the chain was owned by a family from Hong Kong. Finally, Chang began to slow his motorcycle down in front of Succun's home, on the eastside of Phnom Penh.

At first, on seeing his home from the outside, I assumed that he was living in an apartment, but Chang explained to me that it was Succun's and his mother's apartment building, and that the land all around it was all theirs as well. At first, when Succun opened the door, he stood in shock when he recognized me. He did not say anything at first as I stood there and grinned. He did not know what had happened to me, or where I had come from. He welcomed me into his home warmly with a big hug. He had married since I last saw him, and he was also a father, with two sons. His angular jaw and friendly smile were just the same as before, just a few years older. It just seemed that life was playing a funny trick for both of us. The thick, dark hair he once had, was now thinned out more and even graying. He looked the same, just a little older and wiser, as he always worked so hard as I remembered. It was amazing to me, how in a flash, I began to realize how much I should come to expect that many things have changed during my absence. Yet the very wide, thick walls of distance and time that separated me from my friends and family in Cambodia were beginning to dissolve at that moment, as he was the first of anyone from my old life that I was able to meet again. I had not communicated with him for fourteen years, as I did not have his address, and he had no way to know of where I went after getting to Thailand. I must have seemed a little nervous and tense, as I explained the situation of having to wait for the flight down to Battambang to see my family. He remembered me quite well and insisted that I stay with him for the next couple of days and meet his wife and sons while I waited for my flight to northwest Cambodia. His investments had paid off well, as I learned. He no longer had to work as much, as the people he hired managed his trading business for him. When I walked into his apartment, I could see that his two boys were playing video games on the big-screen TV in the living room. Succun introduced his children to me as their Uncle Tha. I was also introduced to his wife. I was surprised with the electronic equipment and nice furniture that they had in their privately owned apartment in the city. We sat down in the living room and just talked for hours. He was delighted to see me, as I was delighted to see him. That night, we had a large dinner spread. Chang, Succun, and some other friends of Succun came over for dinner.

During the day, we discussed what had transpired for both of us over the past fourteen years. His story left off where he had restarted his trading activities, soon after I had left to go to the refugee camp in Thailand. Over the following two years, he had saved enough money to purchase the apartment building and central city lot, jointly with his father-in-law in 1984. The land became so valuable over the following ten years, that he was able to lease part of his lot out to a travel company that used it as a parking lot. He received about US$3,000 per month for his lease, an incredible sum for a family to live on, in Cambodia. In addition, Succun continued his trading business, not in buses or on ships over the Tonle Sap, but instead, on six semi-trucks, that he now owned from mass-hauling goods from the Thai-Cambodian border to Phnom Penh, and from the wholesale markets in Svay Reing to the capital city. On his land, he owned a small apartment complex, where some of his truck drivers lived. Succun insisted on treating me to food, and he also offered me some money. I thanked him, declining the money, but readily accepted his wife's cooking, as she made things for us throughout the day.

We spent many hours that day sharing memories and catching up. He did not have to work that week, so we spent two days together looking around the city. He took me to Tamao, a temple on a small mountain outside of the city. During the cooler periods of the day, we searched for some of my other old friends, but we could not locate any of them, other than some of Malradi's family ...

The plane touching down in Phnom Penh woke me out of my sweet reverie about my visit with Succun and his family. At about 11:30 a.m., I walked into the arrival area of Phnom Penh International Airport, once again, where Tha In and his younger half-brother, Mab, were waiting for me. This time I decided to try a different hotel that I saw when I was looking around Phnom Penh the week before. I stayed at a hotel called Bopah Teep Hotel—meaning rose from heaven hotel. I paid in advance for the entire week, US$70. It was very cheap but very nice. It was right across the street almost from the much more expensive Cambodiana Hotel, which cost about US$80 per night. I wanted to save my money for doing other things while staying in Phnom Penh.

I would not be able to see Succun on my return visit, as he already planned to be away for the week in Thailand on business. Instead, Mab, who was an English teacher at a private school in Phnom Penh, agreed to show me around that week. I paid him in advance as well, as I wanted to make sure that he was happy doing it. I paid him US$100. I also practiced English with him all week to help him, as he did not have that many opportunities to do this with foreigners living in Phnom Penh. It was more of a gift of what I gave him than actual pay, as it was way beyond what was expected. I also paid for his hotel in advance because I was afraid that I would run out of money by the time the week was over, with shopping, eating, or sightseeing expenses.

I was very happy with the hotel, and I decided that I would stay there again during future visits. The room came with two double beds, a refrigerator, TV with remote, bathtub with hot and cold running water, and a desk. I know that in America, this is standard, but not necessarily so in Cambodia. There were no signs on the wall that said "No Hand Grenades or Machine Guns" near the "No Smoking Signs" that I had seen frequently in the International Hotel I stayed at in Battambang and Sisophon. It was near the Grand Palace Complex as well. The floor was covered in a beautiful mosaic of gray and white flower patterns. The cost for cleaning an entire set of clothes down to the underwear and socks was fifty cents, the same as it was in Battambang. This price also covered the pressing and ironing.

After getting settled again in my hotel room, Tha In, Mab, and I went to the Pen Lock, a very nice and very expensive restaurant for Phnom Penh. The outdoor tables offered a panoramic view of the Mekong River in the area near the Grand Palace. The tables there were made of a beautiful, thick hardwood. On the backs of the chairs, there were carvings of Angkor pictorials, as well as scenes from the *Reamker*. We always sat outside when we went there, as there was air-conditioning on the balcony as well. The waiters and waitresses could all speak a variety of languages. They would alternate between English, French, Thai, and of course, Cambodian, with different guests. I often gave them a dollar tip, for which they profusely thanked me. Their monthly pay, being about US$40 per month, including tips, made my tipping seem grandiose. They were extremely gracious with my friends and me, as they came to know me as a big tipper.

I would usually order rice soup, *bahgong,* or *me cha,* with a beer. Everything was just like a Western restaurant, but also very Cambodian. The waiters and waitresses were always attentive, quickly refilling our beer and water glasses after each sip. As we sat and talked, while we ate, we could also look out over the street below and the river. We could look quite away into the distance, as the area around Phnom Penh is quite flat. The tallest building in Phnom Penh is about eight stories in height—the Bank of Hong Kong, the place I would go later that day to find many other foreigners doing the same as me, withdrawing money from my credit card or their savings accounts. There were no buildings of comparable height blocking our view. Lunch for all three of us on that first day back was about US$13. It was so nice and yet so inexpensive.

After lunch, Tha In said goodbye. I would not see him until the last day for my ride back to the airport. Mab stayed with me, and we were soon off to the Riverside Park, a park along the Mekong River. There were many casinos there, along fairgrounds, and an outdoor concert hall, where live music was performed. There were many beautiful flowers along the paved walkway, with the occasional coconut tree. It was best to go there at sunset, where spectacular views could be seen, while walking along or sitting at park benches that were scattered along the long stretch of the park. In the evening time, when I walked along there with Mab, I always had to wear mosquito repellent, as the mosquitoes would like to come out there as well.

On that first day of sightseeing through the park, I told Mab about how I used to go there all the time with my friends, fourteen years before. Succun and Malradi used to go there with me, sometimes with Lim, Ain, or other friends. Although I was only thirteen to sixteen years old when I frequented the park before, I sometimes drove a motorcycle through the roadway in the park. Driver's licenses were non-existent in post-war Cambodia, so even though I was so young, I would still be able to go riding. I sometimes rode on the back with older friends driving. Most of my friends at that time were much older than I, so at the time of my revisit, they were probably in their late thirties and early forties. Mab said that it must have been nice to have had such a nice life in Phnom Penh, when I was so young, and that now it was really wonderful that I have been able to build a life for myself in America as well.

While Mab and I walked along, he asked me many questions about life in America. He also told me about his current situation, which was difficult. After his mother died, his father remarried a woman who was not all that kind to him and his younger brother and sisters. Mab earned about US$50 per month, teaching English, while he also attended the university. He still lived at home with his father and stepmother. His story saddened me when I learned of how his stepmother made him and his little sister and brother sit on the floor during meals, while her natural son, sat at the table with her and his father. How his father could be so uninterested in his natural children, I could not understand. The stepmother's natural son received three meals a day, whereas Mab and his two younger siblings only received one. It was up to Mab to cover the expense of his own schooling, and the expense of food for his younger sister, brother, and himself. This prevented him from being able to move out of his father's house, because he was concerned that his younger sister and brother, who were too young to work, would go hungry with an unconcerned stepmother. Tha In and his family lived about fifty kilometers away from Phnom Penh, in another city, so he was a bit removed from Mab's problems. Yet, Tha In had difficulties of his own as well. I was glad to have been so generous with Mab, giving him US$100. I am sure that it went to good use.

Both Mab and I got to know one of the drivers at the hotel quite well during my stay. He was more than eager to be hired to drive us all over the city in one of the hotel cars. His name was Tear, the same name as my eldest nephew. I paid about US$15 per day to be chauffeur-driven around the city, plus I paid for his meals, as I always invited him to hang out with us. Tear, Mab, and I ended up hanging out together during most of my stay. Tear lived in the city with his mother. His home situation was much better than Mab's. Both of them made very friendly and fun companions during my stay. Tear was very skillful in getting around the city and knowing the best routes to go for visiting different places. It would not be a good idea to expect to drive oneself, as the traffic was bizarre. With the lax traffic rules, we were surprised that we did not see accidents every day. We all witnessed one really bad motorcycle accident, where a couple who was riding on a motorcycle were thrown several meters, and their motorcycle flew about thirty meters before it finally slid to a stop. The man, who thought that his wife was killed, tried to run toward her in the middle of the street, but the man could not stand up with his broken leg. Luckily, she wasn't killed, and she was able to get up. Thankfully none of the fast moving vehicles in the intersection had run over her. After seeing her husband on the side of the street, she ran to him, yelling for someone to help them. People were there to assist them right away. We had just missed the accident, but we needed to move our car as traffic began to get blocked. Many people did not have driver's licenses, especially people who drove from the countryside into the city. People often drove way too fast and sometimes recklessly down the roads. If one were to rent a car without a driver, it would be too easy to get into an accident and get blamed as a foreigner, ending up owing the rental business damages for the car. Insurance was a foreign concept, and for good reason. It was best to stay off the roads, when at all possible.

Our daily ritual usually started with breakfast and then a walk through the market. Then we would have lunch at Pen Lok, followed by an afternoon nap or TV viewing indoors during the high heat of the afternoon. Tear would normally knock on our doors at about 7:00 a.m. each morning, and off we all went for breakfast in the market. We usually had noodle soup which was my favorite for breakfast. Breakfast at the cheaper outdoor restaurants came to usually US$2 for three of us. It was comfortable to eat at these restaurants during the early morning hours, before the temperature started to rise too much.

We would then walk around one of the three main markets in the city. All of them had changed so much since the time that I lived there. The Olympic Market, known also as the wholesale market from before, where I sold my wares, had been torn down and rebuilt. In the years after I had left, the land had been sold to a Hong Kong investor. There was now a three-story mega market with elevators and escalators in its place. I found out from my friend Mab that the first-floor merchants had to pay about US$1,000 per month for a booth to keep their business there. On the top floor, the price fell to around US$800 per month. The first floor was more expensive, as fewer people went upstairs. As the rental prices had become increasingly expensive for the merchants, only about half of the booths there were rented by wholesalers anymore. Many of the wholesalers began to sell their wares from the first floor of their own homes within the city instead. The New Central Market, or *Samutai*, the Cambodian name, was probably my favorite market. This market had a high ceiling, which allowed the cooler breeze to blow through and the heat to also rise as the temperatures increased during the day. It seemed generally cooler there than in the other markets. The New Central Market is not really new, as its name seems to indicate, but has been around for many, many years. It was closed down for several years, from 1975 until about 1982, about the time I left for Thailand. There were maybe as many as one thousand different booths there, where merchants would sell an incredibly wide variety of goods. At both the Olympic and Samutai markets, all kinds of things could be purchased. Everything from cameras, camcorders, sarongs, Buddha statues, and kitchen sinks could be purchased. The array of goods was amazing. I purchased a few souvenirs for friends back in Seattle. I saw the same exact camera for sale at Samutai that I had just purchased in America two weeks before. I purchased the camera, for what I thought was a good deal, for about US$195 in the United States. The same camera in the market sold for US$125 in Cambodia. It did not appear to be fake, or used. One of the main reasons for the difference in price was the much lower taxes and tariffs placed on goods imported into Cambodia. I saw many different ornamental objects as well. If a person wanted to buy a small Buddha statue, it could not be taken through Thailand, as it would be confiscated by the Thai customs. Thailand has a law concerning the transportation of Buddha statutes to protect the possibility of the black market selling true antique treasures removed from different sacred sites in the region. However, if a person returned through Singapore, as I planned to do, a person could take one back to America if one wanted to do so. As the metallic statues were so ubiquitous in the markets, the cheaper quality ones could be purchased for a few cents.

The third market is the *Olusai Market*. My sister Lye Lye told me that my friend Juu still worked there, so Mab and I walked around that market one day to see if we could find her. Lye Lye told me that she and her husband sold vegetables and fruits there. Finally, after searching through many booths we found her. Juu, not recognizing me, asked, "Something you want to buy?" I told her that I was looking for a friend that I had not seen for a long time, and her name is Juu. She looked at me for a while and said, "Put Toh!" with surprise—the Cambodian equivalent to "Oh my God, I can't believe it!" She was so surprised to see me again. I stayed there for about an hour with her. She was very busy, but she insisted that I stay and talk with her. She wanted to meet with me later in the week, although she only had a couple of free hours each day. I decided not to meet with her, as she was so busy with her work, and she needed the time to be with her children. I gave her a little money though, as a gift. Olusai is another big market, with many booths similar to Samutai and the Olympic Market. They were the largest of the markets in the city.

I spoke mainly English, as it gave Mab a chance to practice. Each day, although we followed pretty much the same routine, we did vary our schedule by going to some of the different sites around the capital city. I was fortunate that Mab just happened to be off for two weeks, for New Year's vacation, so he was completely free to show me around. On one of the first days, the three of us, Mab, Tear, and I went to the *Kinswai* Fairgrounds, about a forty-five-minute drive from the hotel, just outside the city. Kinswai was famous for its floating huts that one could rent for the day. There were about one hundred huts, all connected to narrow boardwalks that extended out into the river. Most of the huts did not float but were built on very tall stilts above the water. Others which did float on the water were much more expensive. I rented one of the more expensive floating huts for the day. Mab and Tear were thrilled, as this was something neither of them would be able to afford on their own. Everything was very nice and clean in the hut. Several Cambodian women, all dressed up in traditional clothes waited on us immediately. We stayed there all day talking, inside the hut, riding the soft current up and down, while attached to the narrow boardwalk. It was very relaxing and enjoyable. The whole experience was very unique. After a few drinks, it became even more interesting. As the hut was on the water, it stayed fairly cool, even without a fan or air-conditioning. We ate and drank throughout the day, talking about many things.

Mab and Tear asked me many questions about America. They wanted to know what it was like to live there. They also talked about the current situation in Cambodia. They both wanted the growing tension to subside and for both sides in the government to get along. That would make life easier for everyone. They were very curious about the many rules and laws in America that I kept talking about. I explained how America seemed, at times, to have too many laws and rules, but I explained that the laws were also good, in that they protected the people as well. In Cambodia, the lack of laws made it very difficult for the common people, because people in the government could keep stealing from them, as in the case of my father and his land. As another easier example, the lack of traffic laws resulted in so many traffic accidents. I explained about the busy Seattle traffic, and how the laws provided more safety and organization for so many to live more easily in a large city. The rules allowed for many more cars to actually operate on the road at the same time. In Phnom Penh, the traffic rules would have to get better and be enforced for the city to ever be able to tolerate more congestion. We talked about many topics, and they were in awe with my stories about America. They both hoped that Cambodia would soon develop like other countries, and one day, become more like America. We enjoyed our time together in the floating hut and stayed there until the next afternoon. I highly recommend this place as an unusual place to go. Most of the foreigners who come to Cambodia, get on a plane right away to go to Siem Reap to see Angkor Wat, but there are actually many interesting places to also see right in Phnom Penh. I spent about US$22 for the use of the hut and all of the food and drinks that we had for the entire day, for all three of us. For a Cambodian, this would be the equivalent of spending US$500 for the afternoon—something that only the very rich could afford, as US$22 was equal to about half a month's wages for an average Cambodian at the time.

In the evenings, we would meet at about 9:00 p.m. and stay out until about 1:30 a.m. or 2:00 a.m. in the hotel's lounge and dance bar. It was a lot of fun, as there were seven or eight live soloists singing Cambodian songs. They also had a very nice speaker system for dancing too. They played some popular, recently released songs from America as well. The place was packed full every night. I was surprised by the large number of people out each night. It was a nice way to wind down after the hot temperatures of the day.

Every day, between Pen Lok and the hotel, we passed the Royal Grand Palace. The palace is very similar in style to the architecture of the Royal Grand Palace in Bangkok. It was closed off to tourists for the time being. King Sihanouk was not residing there at the time, as he had taken up residence in China again, as the two main factions were not getting along with each other in the government. It was rumored that his son, Prince Norodom Ranariddh, the first prime minister, resided in one of the structures in the complex. The second prime minister resided somewhere else. I did not know where. In the evenings, the palace was lit up with lights around the sides of the different buildings in the complex. The closest way to describe it is to compare the lighting to that of the evening lighting of the Parliament building in Victoria, British Columbia. The lights made the palace seem festive at night. Much of the palace grounds had been restored, so it was quite impressive from the street outside the palace walls.

Mab took me to the eastside of the palace, to the street that ran in front of that section. Two days before my arrival in Phnom Penh, a strike had gone on in the city. The laborers were protesting their low wages and for not getting a pay increase from a foreign company that they worked for in the city. Someone threw grenades into the crowd, killing sixteen of the strikers. It ended the strike in a very gruesome way. As the police were not all that organized or effective in finding the culprits to many crimes in the city, the criminal instigator went unpunished. It was terrible to hear about. Mab showed me a spot in the road where one of the grenades blew up. There was only a small hole in the roadway to mark where the explosion had occurred. How sad the situation still was in my native country for many people but vastly better than the time of tyranny under the Khmer Rouge just a few years before.

On another day, Mab and I went to the Tuol Sleng Museum. I had been there before, years before, shortly after it had opened. This museum, best symbolized by the map of Cambodia made from skulls, almost four meters wide and four meters tall, was a horrible place during the tyranny of the Khmer Rouge. It was originally the site of a former elementary school. One day, students were in the classrooms studying, and the next day, it had transformed into a death camp of torture rooms, killing rooms, and other gruesome sights, where innocent people met their fate in the worst imaginable ways. While walking down the open-air hallway, with a view of the courtyard below through the barbed wire, I could almost see the students running or walking to class, almost like a haunted vision. The building was undoubtedly the home for anguishing spirits. Many former students, along with their parents, met their fates there during the bloody revolution. There were many exhibits still on display and paintings on the wall that depicted the horrible tortures that went on there. One of the exhibits showed brick partitions where prisoners were separated from each other. Within the partitions, prisoners were shackled to the floor by their ankles. There was not enough space within the confined partitions to lay down flat, but a person could stand up straight there. Many of the machines that were devised were still on display. It was horrifying to imagine that hatred and the desire to kill could be so embraced by a group of people as to cause these sickening episodes in human history. How could anyone want to hurt someone else so badly, as to torture or maim them in the ways that the Khmer Rouge did, and also kill so many. Many of the things that are recorded in this museum are too ghoulish to put in a book, but people around the world must know about the potential for evil that exists within the human mind. I was glad to leave the museum, but at the same time, I was glad to be able to revisit the place that serves as a monument for so many who were killed during the Cambodian holocaust.

My stay in Cambodia was quickly coming to a close. On the morning of my last day there, I was very sad to say goodbye to my new friends, and I was sad to say goodbye to Cambodia for a while as well. Tha In, his parents, and Mab all saw me off at the airport. I thanked them profusely for their kindness. I was ready to return to Seattle though, as it was almost one month before when I said goodbye to my friends Matt and Seim at SEATAC. It was one of the best months that I had ever had in my life. My flight itinerary was to go to Singapore first, before connecting up with the airline that would take me back to Tokyo-Narita Airport, and then to Seattle.

On the Silk Air flight to Singapore, the many, many memories that I made over the past month went through my mind. My sister Lye Lye had given me some dried mangos to eat on my trip back home, and some more for me to eat back at home. I was looking forward to developing my pictures of my family and seeing my family on the TV through my camcorder upon my return. The flights back were uneventful. I stayed at a hotel that was right in the airport in Singapore to avoid going through Singapore's customs and immigration. I slept very well on the flights back to the United States; it was with some sadness but also with a feeling of contentment that I left Cambodia again for the second time.

On my last flight home, I reminisced about my mother and my stepmother, Lem. I wondered if my mother was still watching over me in a special way to make sure that I was still safe and somehow protected from the crazy challenges that I have continued to face in my life. Also, maybe my stepmother, Lem, was watching over me too. There were many relatives and friends that perished in the holocaust. I wondered where they had really gone, and I hoped that they all found peace, wherever they were. I was so thankful that so many in my family were still alive. One day, it will be our time for passing too, but I would like my story to continue on, so that people will remember and will do what they can to prevent such devastation from ever happening again.

20

A BRIEF HISTORY OF CAMBODIA

My native county has a very ancient history, with Angkor Wat and the Bayon Complex as the main focal points of interest. My small native country of Cambodia is a remnant of a large and prosperous kingdom. According to National Geographic, the metropolis that had once surrounded the ancient UNESCO sites of the Angkor Wat Complex and the Bayon Temple had a population of around 750,000 residents at its height in the thirteenth century, at a time when London had about 150,000.[6] With the use of imaging radar and other tools, researchers have discovered that the central city was made possible by the use of a very sophisticated water system, with man-made aqueducts and canals for storing water during the heavy rains to last them through the very hot and dry seasons. This allowed city residents to have adequate water in the city as well as for agricultural use to support the large population.[7]

While growing up in Sisophon, I had no knowledge of my country's history, nor of how close I lived to a former seat of great power, just one hundred kilometers away. My father often talked about Angkor Wat, and

---

6 Stone, Richard, "Angkor, Why an Ancient Civilization Collapsed," *National Geographic*, p. 36.

7 Ibid., p. 36.

my mother took me there when I was a baby. During my boyhood, I never reflected upon "history." History for me was the year before or the stories and superstitions that I heard while growing up.

Even today, Angkor Wat is the largest religious structure in the world, featuring over a half mile (0.9 kilometers) of stone carvings that describe Indian epics, myths about Vishnu, and events from early Khmer history.[8] A very interesting depiction from the height of its power came from a Chinese envoy, Chou Ta-Kuan, who lived in the capital city of Angkor from 1296 to 1297 and wrote of what he witnessed: "On the king's outings, processions of palace servants, numbering in the hundreds, sometimes reaching a thousand, preceded the entourage, followed by princes and priests riding on ornately decorated elephants. Hundreds of lofty, bright red parasols shadowed the processioners. Following were contingents of troops, with flags and music. At the end, the king, sacred sword in hand, was mounted on his large, ornamented elephant which had golden encased tusks."[9] The envoy also wrote about the festivals that the king and his people celebrated every month. Rockets of fireworks were launched into the nighttime skies and could be seen from a mile away.[10]

The Angkor civilization remained strong until the late 1300s, when wars, and possibly epidemics, brought the empire into decline.[11] Some scholars speculate it was the period of drought from 1362 to 1392 and from 1415 to 1440 that may have exacerbated an already ailing complicated water system, which could have been the beginning of the end times of the great Khmer Kingdom.[12] Other scholars speculate that wars between neighboring kingdoms may have eventually led to the decay of the irrigation systems throughout the country, systems that provided much of the water needed for Cambodia's prosperous food production.

8 Chandler, *The Land and People of Cambodia*, p. 66.

9 Chandler, *A History of Cambodia*, p. 75.

10 Ibid., p. 72.

11 Chandler, *The Land and People of Cambodia*, p. 76.

12 Stone, Richard, "Angkor, Why an Ancient Civilization Collapsed." *National Geographic*, p. 54.

The powerful kingdom of Ayutthaya that rose up nearby, in what is now present-day Thailand, finally drove the Cambodians to move their capital to Phnom Penh in the year 1430, leaving Angkor Wat behind to eventually be forgotten, except by the locals living in the area.[13] Then in the 1860s, Henri Mouhot, a French explorer, rediscovered the lost city of Angkor, after following up on reports of ancient ruins being described near the town of Siem Reap. Mouhot's rediscovery of Angkor Wat enhanced the mystery behind the country's long history. The archeological site provided interesting clues into the history of the region. This massive religious structure, mysteriously hidden away in the jungle for centuries, had been completely out of the knowledge and minds of the rest of the world, until Mouhot's discovery.

The French remained in control of the kingdom, determining the policy for the Cambodian people. The malleable nature of the Cambodian people and the perception of the French as a great and powerful race made the people all the more yielding to French control. The French continued their administration of the kingdom up until WWII. In the early 1940s, the Japanese incorporated Cambodia into its East Asia Co-Prosperity Sphere.[14] In return for Thailand's alliance with the Japanese during WWII, the province of Battambang (where I grew up, and where my mother's family principally lived) and the province or Siem Reap, including Angkor Wat (the area where my father's family was from), were ceded to Thailand.[15] The remainder of the Cambodian Kingdom was kept under nominal control by the French.[16]

In 1941, a new king had to be selected, and the French chose Prince Sihanouk, among several candidates in the Royal Cambodian Family, to become the new king. The stage for the present day conflict was beginning to be set. Succession to the throne never fell necessarily to the eldest son but whomever had the favoritism of the ruling elite, whether it be Khmer, Vietnamese, Thai, or French. Sihanouk began his reign at the very young age of

---

13 Stone, Richard, "Angkor, Why an Ancient Civilization Collapsed.", *National Geographic*, p. 77.

14 Sheehan, *Cambodia*, p. 20.

15 Ibid., p. 20.

16 Ibid., p. 20.

nineteen, fresh from high school, and amenable to the policies of the French, so it was thought. In the few years to follow, Sihanouk went from dealing with the French, to the Japanese, and then back to the French again, until he was able to liberate Cambodia in 1953. Sihanouk, for a period of time, was perceived by the Cambodian public as a type of hero for dealing with the French, and gaining the country's first true independence from foreign powers for the first time in hundreds of years. In 1955, Sihanouk abdicated his throne in favor of his father, Norodom Suramarit. This allowed him to found a political party, the Sangkum, which swept the country in its national elections.[17] He became the prime minister from 1955 to 1960, and again the head of state from 1960, after the death of his father. Sihanouk played a skillful political game throughout the 1950s and 1960s, keeping Cambodia's neutrality between China, the United States, and its allies, and the Soviet Union and Vietnam, saying about Cambodia, "When the elephants fight, the grass is trampled,"[18] referring to the country's small size and seeming unimportance. In the 1960s, conflicts erupted between a growing tide of communist supporters and the conservatives, breaking into civil war. Sihanouk secretly agreed, after breaking off ties with the United States, in 1965, to allow the Americans to bomb Vietcong positions within the Cambodian borders; however, he later changed his mind after hearing reports of extensive bombings up and down the eastern border.[19] In 1970, Sihanouk had lost much of his earlier popularity, and public protests were staged against his rule. While he was abroad in Paris, the National Assembly voted him out of office. The thousand-year monarchy was abolished. General Lon Nol, the prime minister at the time who supported American efforts against the Vietnamese communists, took control of the country. During the following five years, a full-scale civil war mounted across the countryside. At the same time, American B-52s carpet-bombed the countryside in an attempt to wipe out

17 Chandler, *A History of Cambodia*, p. 117.

18 Ibid., p. 118–120.

19 Steinberg, *In Search of Southeast Asia, a Modern History*, p. 378.

Vietcong strongholds within the Cambodian border area and later against communist groups within the country as well.

Sihanouk, in an attempt to reclaim his power, established a coalition government with Beijing, where he allied his forces in Cambodia with the small militant group, the Khmer Rouge, a group he had earlier belittled as "a petty army of rebels."[20] Mao Zedong's China supported the Khmer Rouge and Sihanouk's attempt to reclaim power in Cambodia. Civil war broke out over much of Cambodia, especially in the south and east. Lon Nol's air force dropped napalm on villages and suspected encampments behind communist lines. The carpet bombings of the Americans and Lon Nol's forces brought about a tide of resentment and extreme animosity among the survivors, causing many to enlist to fight with the communists with vengeance in their hearts.[21] During the Cambodian civil war, the United States spent US$7 billion on aerial bombings over the country.[22] Unfortunately, many innocent civilians, who were caught up in the war being fought on their land, were also among those being bombed. The Western public was initially kept unaware of the intense bombings of the Cambodian countryside, as many of the original documents ordering these secret American raids, without the approval of Congress, were shredded.[23] More than twice the tonnage of bombs were dropped on Cambodia in this undeclared war, than on Japan during WWII.[24]

When the Americans pulled out of Vietnam and stopped offering support to General Lon Nol, the general's resources became depleted. In April 1975, Phnom Penh fell to the Khmer Rouge, and then Saigon fell to the North Vietnamese thirteen days later. The leader of the Khmer Rouge, Pol Pot, put Sihanouk under house arrest at his palace. Sihanouk was not to be a part of the new revolutionary scheme, although he gave the Khmer Rouge the much needed support to attain victory. Pol Pot (formerly known as Saloth Sar, a

---

20 Ibid., p. 378.

21 Kiernan, *How Pol Pot Came to Power*, p. 351.

22 Shawcross, *Sideshow: Kissinger, Nixon and the Destruction of Cambodia*, p. 350.

23 Ibid., p. 350.

24 Steinberg. *In Search of Southeast Asia*, p. 379.

school teacher) established a communist system, entirely unique to Cambodia. Immediately, all citizens were told to evacuate and leave the cities for fear of US bombing raids—raids that were not really expected by the Khmer Rouge leadership. It was a ploy to totally reorganize Cambodian society and to weed out all opposition to the new regime. During the following three years eight months and twenty days, two million Cambodian people died in the worst holocaust in Asian history. Khmer Rouge villages were set up, and a forced labor was instituted on the population. Thus, the political situation that so shaped my life from an early age took hold of the country.

Cambodian culture was almost completely wiped out, as almost all of the intellectuals and educated population were executed. It has been theorized that if Cambodia had succumbed to the revolutionaries in 1973, before the most intense American bombing raids, instead of in 1975, the CPK (Communist Party of Kampuchea) would not have had the precedent to evacuate people into the countryside from the cities.[25] The evacuation of so many smaller towns in 1973, as a result of the American bombing raids, set the precedent that was to be used in the major evacuations of Phnom Penh and Battambang in 1975.[26] It was very believable that raids would soon occur, so the Khmer Rouge were able to influence people to leave their homes and most of their belongings behind, as scare tactics, making them believe that they would be able to return within three days.[27] Of course, no one was allowed to return, and many of their homes were ransacked while they were away. This forced evacuation was part of Pol Pot's scheme to totally restructure the Cambodian society and weed out Khmer Rouge. To dumb down the population and keep it controlled was an underlying, driven directive in their philosophy, to base the new society on a radical new concept of living, uncharted and untested. This teacher with extremely novel viewpoints came to power, and the true ideas were not really understood by the population at large. They wanted to put society on its head and start anew with no reflec-

25 Kiernan, *How Pol Pot Came to Power*, p. 390–391.
26 Ibid., p. 391.
27 Kiernan, *How Pol Pot Came to Power*, p. 390–391.

tion onto the past. The assumption was that no one from within the country would have the wit to challenge the leadership. The displacement of the entire population put the Cambodian people completely at the mercy of the Khmer Rouge soldiers. It was Pol Pot's strategy to organize the entire country into collectivized units in an attempt to increase countrywide productivity—all in the name of nationalism and independence. It was felt that this Maoist precept would create a powerful agrarian economy that could more easily fend off foreign invaders in the future. Pol Pot's plan called for "A Super Great Leap Forward."[28] Unfortunately, Pol Pot's ideology did not match the Cambodian reality. He forgot that Cambodians were human, with a very strong spiritual tradition embedded with a proud word-of-mouth history and appreciation for humanity. Pol Pot's ideology was that of equating humans to horses, or more like robots without the need for food and human bonding. He thought we, as Cambodians, could be used only for production and bettering the state, or the "Angkar," the Communist Party of Kampuchea. There is no accurate account of how many people perished, but a figure of about two million is generally accepted.[29]

As a result of Pol Pot's regime, these people died from the initial displacement, hardship in the Khmer Rouge villages, or the tortuous executions. It was a very dark time for Cambodia. The revolutionary group that many Cambodians casually, and sometimes fanatically, supported, did not protect them from the evils that they felt were rooted in the Americans, the Sihanoukist, the Vietnamese, and other foreign powers. Instead, they found themselves brought into slavery by a regime that many assisted in bringing to power. Others who were totally uninvolved in the war, found themselves uprooted from home and family; many were lost, never to be heard from again. The fighting did end, yet life changed for most Cambodians into a forced day-to-day imprisonment filled with fear and heartache. The problems were exacerbated by the uneducated and entirely untrained troops that were put in charge of the controlled villages throughout the country. The old way

28 Chandler, *The Land and People of Cambodia*, p. 136.
29 Shawcross, *The Quality of Mercy*, p. 331.

of life was destroyed, and the country was in the hands of an uneducated elite, strung together by an untested ideology that could only lead to despair and destruction of the spirit. The cruelty of Pol Pot's ideology is best exhibited at the Tuol Sleng Museum in Phnom Penh, a place where torturous persecutions and vicious executions were carried out daily, first toward the citizens of the city, and later, to supposed-traitors within the ranks of the CPK itself.

In 1978, the Vietnamese communists allied themselves with Heng Samrin and Samdech Hun Sen, two Cambodian generals, in an attempt to oust Pol Pot from power. In January 1979, they succeeded, returning Cambodia to a moderately peaceful state of affairs after such a long period of turmoil and bloodshed. The arriving troops discovered the enslaved village workers in encampments first-hand, much to their disbelief. The emaciated appearance of the villagers also testified to the cruelty of the CPK and its leadership. Even after the Vietnamese-supported forces overran the country, the Khmer Rouge persisted in rural strongholds and continued to menace the common people by laying down landmines at night in the countryside, especially along roads or near train lines. Cambodian refugees traveled to borders, uncertain of Vietnamese control and with fear in their hearts of a Khmer Rouge revival.

The Vietnamese communists were actually seen as heroes to the Cambodian people at first, rescuing them from the evil Khmer Rouge. Yet, in the years that followed the 1978 coup, stability was precarious, as guerilla warfare began in the rural provinces. Approximately, seven million landmines[30] were laid down by both the Khmer Rouge and various government-supported factions in an attempt to imperil each other's soldiers. This continued until 1996, when the Khmer Rouge forces were neutralized by defectors for the most part. As a result, the people of Cambodia were the ones who bore the brunt of the hostilities, as many farmers, or people in the general population, unknowingly walked over landmines, causing loss of limbs or life. International efforts had been established to rid the country of these weapons, yet the number of landmines, as well as the problem of discovering their locations, make the efforts to clean up the countryside slow

30 Sheehan, *Cambodia*, p. 55.

and tedious. It is estimated that one service worker is killed for every 5,000 landmines that are found and destroyed.[31]

In 1993, the United Nations (UN) mounted its largest and most costly peace operation in Cambodia, the master plan of the Paris Peace Accords of 1991. At the cost of US$2 billion, appropriated by the UN, over 23,000 troops, as well as 1,400 officials from other countries were brought in, to establish free elections and to enforce authority.[32] As part of the plan, 360,000 refugees, who had been living in Thailand, were safely repatriated to Cambodia, and 50,000 Cambodians were trained by the UN to work in the election process. Out of an estimated 9.6 million people, 4.8 million were registered to vote, and among those, 90 percent cast ballots.[33]

"The three parties that won most of the seats in the 120 seat assembly, were the following: (1) FUNCINPEC—the Royalist party, the National United Front for an Independent, Neutral, Peaceful and Cooperative Cambodia (58 seats); (2) CPP—the party that represented the former Vietnamese-backed government, named the Cambodia Peoples Party (51 seats); and (3) BLDP—a non-communist group, called the Buddhist Liberal Democratic Party (10 seats)."[34] Cambodia became, once again, a kingdom, with a representative assembly. Sihanouk was reinstated as king. The leader of FUNCINPEC, Sihanouk's son, Prince Ranariddh, became the new prime minister. Hun Sen, the leader of the CPP, and a war hero, refused to step down from power, as the election results were close. He was concerned about instability, without a strong hand on the current military. To prevent the possibility of another civil war, King Sihanouk was able to engender a political agreement between the two leaders, in a co-premiership. Ranariddh would be the first prime minister and Hun Sen would be the second prime minister. Many were skeptical of the new government. Hun Sen, controlling the military, and with

31 Lamb, Kate, "Mission Impossible: U.N. in Cambodia Showed Early Limits of Nation Building," *Reuters* (Brussels), June 27, 1997.

32 Sheehan, *Cambodia*, p. 27.

33 Ibid., p. 28.

34 Sheehan, *Cambodia*, p. 28.

disgust toward the monarchy, was feared to be ready to topple all of the work of the UN, making the US$2 billion investment meaningless. Ranariddh, a trained lawyer in international law, did not have the military experience to challenge Hun Sen.

The Khmer Rouge did what they could to impede the election process. The Khmer Rouge, then calling themselves the KDP (Party of Democratic Kampuchea), threatened to do anything in their power to disrupt the election process, but due to the presence of the UN's peace-keeping forces, the Khmer Rouge were able to do little to impede the electoral process. The Khmer Rouge did not put forth any candidates of their own, which inevitably created doubt to their real power for future elections. Trained to fight only with weapons, an elected assembly was not a place for them to fight, or to create influence.

Immediately after the elections, First Prime Minister Ranariddh used the Cambodian Army to fight an offensive against the remnants of the Khmer Rouge guerila force. Many Khmer Rouge soldiers defected, switching sides to Ranariddh or Hun Sen. Despite the attempt to eradicate the Khmer Rouge completely, they have continued on, holding onto their bizarre ideas. Unfortunately, the shared objective of dismantling the Khmer Rouge forces was one of the few areas of agreement between the two rival premiers. Soon after the new coalition government was created, animosities began to grow between Ranariddh and Hun Sen. Hun Sen still remained in control of the largest portion of Cambodia's military. Despite the rivalry, the country entered a relatively peaceful period. In 1997, disagreements began to heat up. In late March of 1997, a strike protesting the low wages of a foreign-owned company in Phnom Penh was broken up with a grenade attack in the city. It was rumored in Phnom Penh, among friends, while I was there, that the violence was somehow linked to the growing trend toward violence among the rival leaders. Also, the month before, a TV station that had leanings toward one of the leaders was attacked by the opposition party while "on air." Several people were injured and some killed. It was still discussed in the newspapers there, while I was there.

Later that year, Madeleine Albright, the Secretary of State for the United States, decided to cancel her planned visit to Phnom Penh, scheduled for June 28, 1997, citing security concerns. A refugee herself, it was disappointing to know that she would not go to Phnom Penh, but I completely understood. Tensions were high, and I could feel it, while I was visiting there that year, in April of 1997. American intelligence was quite accurate because they calculated correctly that the rivalry between the two co-premiers could not be mitigated. The political tensions culminated into a coup d'état from July to September, just a little more than two months after I returned home from my visit there. It was a dangerous time.

To summarize very briefly, General Hun Sen eventually became the head of government and remained so until his retirement in 2023, when his son Hun Manet became the country's new prime minister, or head of government. In October 2004, Norodom Sihamoni, Ranariddh's brother, was crowned King of Cambodia and continues to be the head of state today. He is a bachelor with no heirs. At his eventual passing, a new king will be selected from the Cambodian Royal Throne Council one day. Basically, executive power is exercised by the council of ministers, headed by the prime minister, with the consent of the monarch.

With rough periods of political infighting, sometimes with soldier skirmishes, Cambodia has found a path forward. To the relief of many of my Cambodian friends, who also were refugees like me, they have been able to return home and visit their families from time to time. The infusion of Cambodian people into America is one of the reminders that America is a country of immigrants, one that allows for a safe haven to those from areas of the world where serious clashes have occurred. When I was young, a boy growing up in Sisophon, not in my wildest dreams would I have guessed that I would have ended up living in Seattle, Washington. It is my hope that although the fragile peace continues in Cambodia, the country will regain its prosperity and cultural heritage once again.

EPILOGUE

YEARS LATER, THE YEAR 2023

Years later, I was walking through the British Museum in London, the Egyptian Exhibit no less, and suddenly I reminisced about Sisophon, Phnom Penh, and how far my life has come in general since the days of living in Cambodia. I knew it was time to pull the manuscript off the shelf, dust it off, and renew it, and finally publish it. My friend Matt and I had put it together in parts over the past thirty years, but it hasn't been easy to share all the stories with strangers of what I had gone through. Part of it was shame, and part of it was just that the stories were still too hard to share. During the Khmer Rouge forced labor camps, in the blink of an eye, I could have been pulled aside and taken away, if someone felt I was disobedient, or if someone simply did not like me. So many others died. I survived, and out of love for those friends who did not survive the dark days of the Khmer Rouge, and for the trauma experienced by my family, I owe it to them to share our experiences with the world. I am glad for the many books published on the topic of genocide that happened in Cambodia, as it is a memoir of people's true life experiences of what can happen when evil takes over in the worst possible way.

I have been blessed and lucky in so many ways, not a wealthy man, but comfortable in my middle-age years, first for having survived so much in my youth, and then having had the opportunity to travel the world, to walk around the old buildings in Rome, to walk on the wall of Dubrovnik, to walk the streets of Paris, to watch the Formula One race in downtown Budapest on May Day, and to watch Tango dancing on the streets of Buenos Aires, Argentina. I live in a nice, comfortable home now in Seattle, and although I live there, because of my cultural differences, I am still misunderstood by people. They do not know how I came to acquire it, or anything really. My English language pronunciation is still not the best, but I have worked hard with my spouse during our different careers, and we have saved and invested well. Some people overlook me because I do not speak English perfectly, and I am getting older. Some people assume that I am not smart.

When I look at the ancient artifacts in the British Museum, I am reminded about how much time goes by, and how many stories are lost to the wind. I want the world to know my family's story. In Cambodia, we did not have very much, but the love for my family was what helped me survive, as well as the love for my friends and animals, when I was younger. I was beyond lucky by any measure. I have been fortunate for the love in my life, and for my spouse. If I can offer advice to anyone, it is to be kind and to love much and love often. Be a friend by helping another person solve a problem. Share your food, as it is like sharing life and sustenance. Spend as much time with your loved ones as you can, as none of us are here forever.

My father passed away nearly seventeen years ago. My sister Paht called me on the phone, with my sister Lye Lye from a cell phone the family acquired. It was before FaceTime or the technology of today where you can readily see each other on the phone. They were crying. It was so expensive for them to call me. My father had just passed away, and they wanted to let me know right away. My voice that came over the phone loudly, caused movement in my father although the doctor had pronounced him dead hours before. His hand moved up toward his head and his mouth appeared to open, although he had passed. And it was his lifeless body there. My sisters cried as they knew how much my father wanted to see me one more time before he passed. He had a terrible time in his last few months, and Paht was troubled for not being able to move him around easily. They checked his pulse, and there was no pulse, but a body memory from his soul, reached out to say goodbye, my sisters said. I was in shock and continued to speak into the phone, hoping it would cause more movement, but there was none. My father was gone after eighty-two years of life, and in Cambodia, considering what he survived, it was a miracle many times over.

My brother, Vuutey, passed away last year, and because of the COVID-19 pandemic, I was not able to travel there to attend the funeral rites. I was in Puerto Vallarta. The sail monument in Puerto Vallarta looked just like the funeral pyre for my brother in the pictures. I will never see that monument the same way again. I missed out on seeing several of his fellow officers standing guard at his funeral, and his son, Oun, shaving his head in respect to honor his father, as he began his duty of a year of service to be a monk at the nearby temple. I could only send them money and visit on social media, but I could not fly there and attend the funeral. Masks were required and COVID-19 spread in the villages quickly. The travel restrictions in place made it impossible for me to travel to Sisophon to say my last goodbyes to my cherished brother.

I was fortunate to make three trips back to Cambodia, and even brought my friend Matt with me. It was very interesting for him. When he arrived in Bangkok to buy a ticket to fly over to Siem Reap, the border was closed due to riots happening in Phnom Penh over statements a Thai actress made on TV about Angkor Wat. Luckily, just as suddenly as the border closed, it reopened, and Matt was able to buy a ticket at the airport for the one-hour flight to Siem Reap. The plane was filled with media people in hopes of getting to Phnom Penh by train, or on another flight inside Cambodia. As soon as they landed, the border closed down again. My sister Lye Lye and my nieces, Saphon and Sah, came with me and met Matt on the other side of customs in Cambodia. Matt was surprised how similar Lye Lye looked to me—but with long hair, he said. We did not pay attention to the border closing, as we planned to be there for three weeks, and likely it would reopen again soon, we felt.

We spent the next several days touring Angkor Wat and enjoying the quietude of Siem Reap, before making the journey to Sisophon. We made the journey by hired bus to Sisophon. The highway was a dirt highway in most places, or just gravel. Highway 6 was not really paved yet, but they were working on this with grants from different governments. In two areas where ravines that were three or four feet wide, the property owner would wait by the side of the road, and for a few coins, he would put wood down for the van to cross so that we could continue on in our journey. It was still very undeveloped. I pointed out to Matt the general area of the first Khmer Rouge village where I had lived, where I had been punished for stealing the cob of corn. Highway 6 came very close to the Gokpanro village where I was forced to work, until I fled to my aunt's village, at Oambel. The areas were quite barren when we drove through them, but I knew the coordinates in my mind as I gauged how far we were from Sisophon.

When we got to Sisophon, my sisters Paht and Pah did not know I was coming there. When she saw the van, I could literally feel her emotion and tears, as could Matt, from thirty meters away. She came running to greet us and had a huge smile with her large white teeth. She cried and was so happy. Then word spread among the village, and about eighty-eight of my nieces and nephews descended on us, all giving us hugs. This included grand-nieces and grand-nephews now. I brought US$20 bills to give to them, as I knew I would greet many of them. I had to make sure I gave something to each of them, so they would not be crushed in disappointment. It was a lot of cash I carried back home in small change. My older sister Pah came over and greeted us. They were surprised by Matt, as they had only heard of my friend in America, but they did not know how big he was. My nephews and nieces were quite shy and gathered around. Then my father was pushed over in his wheelchair. It was so hot. Matt and I were sweating through our shirts as the heat was quite high with very high humidity. Pah kept fanning Matt, worried that he might pass out, but he was strong. We sat under my father's small house, with its twelve-foot-high stilts supporting it above us. It was cooler under the shade of the house. I talked while Matt just smiled as he didn't speak very much Cambodian except for "Soks abye jeehateh?" or "How are you?" We then went up into the hut and sat and talked. Some of the nephews and nieces were quite shy but they wanted to say "hello." It was decided that we will go to the International Hotel nearby. The cost was US$15 per night. They had air-conditioning. So several of us piled into the room, and we all sat around in there. We stayed for just two days there in Sisophon, until my brother, Vuutey, could arrive with his wife, Toll, and their son.

We decided to return to Siem Reap with a few of my relatives. June and his wife, Succur, and my nephew, Chan, along with both Lye Lye and my nieces Saphon and Sah all squeezed into the van for our ride back to Siem Reap. In Siem Reap, we got three hotel rooms for everyone. We all planned to visit the Angkor Wat complex over three days. Matt had to buy a pass, but for native Cambodians, it was free to go inside. We were surprised as the intermittent border closings deterred many tourists from visiting Angkor Wat at the time. So it was almost as if we were gifted with the opportunity to tour around the entire complex by ourselves, except for a few other tourists. My little nephew, Chan, overcame his shyness, and Matt gave him piggy back rides around much of the complex. Chan was pretty small, so it was easy for Matt to carry him around. Matt did power lifting, so it wasn't a problem. We walked down the front stoned bridge that led into the Angkor Wat complex, and once we entered, it was quiet and serene. It did not seem ghostly as I had imagined it would. There were monks in small groups in different areas of the complex and they agreed to have their picture taken with us. They took pictures of us as well. We gave them donations for their time. In the center column of the complex, the largest and tallest, we all climbed up the very steep, almost vertical stairs to the top. Inside was a small sanctuary, of a small Buddha statue. We all sat around quietly fanning ourselves while in deep contemplation. We looked out through window openings with decorated spindles along the window frames, to the different parts of the ruins below. It was honestly magical to be there with so few people, and several of my relatives at the same time. Lye Lye kept fanning Matt and smiling, wondering how he could take the heat. It was hotter than a Bikram yoga class in there. The stones used to build Angkor Wat were immense and the place was very old. Although we were high up in the structure, it was well-maintained by the monks who frequented the sanctuary. After a while, we were all ready to head down the very steep staircase to the main level. On the back and sides of many of the interior walls were carvings of apsaras, statues of female celestial beings, used as supports for huge stone ceiling ramparts. There were long walls of bas-relief stone carvings that told the stories of many historical events. Very few other tourists were there. My nephew and nieces could run up and down the long corridors without a worry of bothering anyone, and I imagine the spirits didn't mind their cheerful sounds. As the day was quite hot, we all returned to our hotel rooms to rest for the afternoon, and then met up again later, for dinner at the hotel's restaurant. The next day, we all visited the ancient Bayon Temple, with its fifty-four giant face towers, and 216 giant smiling Buddha faces, all looking toward the four cardinal directional points of north, south, east and west. The heads may have originally been representations of the Hindu god, Vishnu, with his four faces. Then later they were adapted to the prevailing religion of the time, to be referred to as Buddha faces, as Buddhism began to replace Hinduism as the dominant religion for the kingdom in later centuries. The heads were massive, and we walked around them, and then down under them, where different Buddhist monks incanted prayers and burned incense. Out of respect, we prayed and put a stick of incense into the large dish of sand that was there and offered a donation under several of the large Buddha heads. The smell was amazing with all of the incense burning, and the smells of something being cooked nearby, outside at a tourist stand. The sounds of birds chirping around the ancient monuments while we were visually taking in the ancient ruins was an explosion to the senses. It was truly an amazing day. It was unforgettable to be there with some of my family as well.

These memories and others of walking in Phnom Penh, along the Riverside Park, with Lye Lye, Saphon, Sah, and Matt were also astounding memories. We decided to get two rooms at the Cambodiana Hotel. Women in one room and men in the other. Mab, who traveled with me before in Phnom Penh, met us and stayed with us during our trip. He could practice his English with Matt and me. The amazing statue of Maitreya, the Buddha of the Future, still stood tall and magnificent in the Buddha Hall, adjacent to the Grand Palace in Phnom Penh. The large diamond on the statue's forehead was amazing, and it almost seemed like his eyes moved to watch us. The tall statute seemed to speak to me that "we would be back there again." It was similar to the tapestries in the Vatican Museum in Rome, where the figures in the tapestries appeared to follow you as you walked across the room. We stood and reflected at the beauty of this tall standing Buddha, which amazingly stood preserved during the course of terrible events of Cambodia's recent past. Luckily, some remnants of our great Cambodian civilization lasted through it all.

I was so glad on this journey to spend so much time with my father back in Sisophon, while waiting for Matt's arrival. I had a chance to talk with him and just be in his presence. It was the last time I was able to see him alive. I did get the chance to talk to him on the phone several times, when Pah or Paht would put the phone up close to his ear. He had trouble hearing in his golden years, and he spoke very little. When he did speak, everyone would listen intently on what he said. I miss my father terribly, and I feel, in some ways, he is now with me always, looking over my shoulder and helping me enjoy my life.

Much of my enjoyment comes from cooking and traveling. Of my travel experiences in Europe, the two that really amazed me was walking around the Acropolis in Athens and visiting the Colosseum in Rome. I thought while walking around these places, *Not in a million years would I have dreamed of going to these places.* From Sisophon to Athens, Rome, or Paris was quite the stretch of the imagination. I very much enjoyed the Buddha restaurant/bar in Paris, near Champs Elysees. I loved the giant Buddha in there.

In Seattle, the town I call home mostly now, there have been many changes. In the past few years, the homeless situation has skyrocketed. I remember coming to America with just my backpack and not really being able to speak English all that well and getting a job right away. It did not pay very much, and through friends, I was blessed with better accommodations. My heart goes out to those in trouble, but my empathy stops when I see them get violent or angry. I can certainly understand the anger at their unfortunate circumstances, but I cannot condone drug experimentation or usage. So many lives are needlessly destroyed, just like the ways the Khmer Rouge randomly picked people and tortured and killed them. It's almost the same way, as drugs will kill you and ruin your life. I always made myself save money when I could, even if it was difficult at times. I did my best to rehabilitate and repurpose furniture and things. I still have my blue pouch where I kept my gold buried in the hut of the refugee camp in those years. I've kept it on our TV as a memory of that time of survival and hope. I will never forget the kindness toward my friend Malradi and me by the older couple that we hid out with for nearly a year in the camp. I appreciated many of my friends who helped me survive at times, when pulling myself up by my own bootstraps didn't really work, since the boots had holes and there were no straps, so to speak. The kindness from Seim and Pah, as well as from Matt, and his family, I have come to appreciate so much. My spouse and I have great gratitude to the many kind people whom we have met on our paths.

As we return home from a wonderful stay in Kensington to my home in Seattle, I know it is time to finally share my story and the story of my family in Cambodia. I do not want their story to go away like dust in the wind, or just be a number among many other stories. I hope it opened your mind and your heart to hear this story, so it does not repeat again and again in history. When teachers or leaders are too extreme, do not immediately follow them to fight for their ideas. Do not follow them into the forest of no return. You do not need to advocate for anyone unless you know them well. In the blink of an eye, society can turn on its head, and you may be the one who ends up being the one taken away, to never be heard from again.

With loving kindness, from my family to yours, Tha Chhay.

March 28, 1988, My new I.D. photo when accepted
and chosen to go to America

Excited and nervous, the day of departing for America,
September 22, 1988

Matthew Raudsepp, co-author, with Tha Chhay's father, Jaik Chhay, 2003

Matt with my nieces and nephews at Angkor Wat, Feb 2003

Matthew Raudsepp & Tha Chhay Alki Beach Apr 2015

Tha Chhay on an airplane to Osaka, Japan, December 2012

Tha Chhay, 3 Days After Being in America, September 1988

Tha Chhay, In his tuxedo, Seattle 1991

**Back side of Angkor Wat, Leaving from the Backdoor
Compliments, Erika MacKay, 1997**

BIBLIOGRAPHY

Chandler, David P., *A History of Cambodia*. Boulder, Colorado: Westview Press, 1983.

Chandler, David P., *The Land and People of Cambodia*. New York: Harper Collins Publishers, 1991.

Kiernan, Ben, *How Pol Pot Came to Power*. London: Verso, 1987.

National Geographic, Richard Stone, "Angkor: Why an Ancient Civilization Collapsed," July 2009.

Reuters News Agency, Lamb, Kate, "Mission Impossible: U.N. in Cambodia Showed Early Limits of Nation Building." (Brussels), June 27, 1997.

Shawcross, William, *The Quality of Mercy*. New York: Simon & Schuster, 1984.

Shawcross, William, *Sideshow: Kissinger, Nixon and the Destruction of Cambodia*. New York: Marshall Cavendish, 1996.

Sheehan, Sean, *Cultures of the World: Cambodia*. New York: Marshall Cavendish, 1996.

Steinberg, David J. (Editor) and David P. Chandler, *In Search of Southeast Asia*. Honolulu: University of Hawaii Press, 1987.

U.S. Committee for Refugees; Refugee Reports. Dec 31, 1994.

SPECIAL ACKNOWLEDGEMENTS

Chhay: Special thanks to the men and women of the United Nations, and the International Red Cross for all of their assistance at the Khao I Dang Refugee Camp. Also to those workers at the U.S. Consulate located near the camp to make conditions better for all of us who waited inside Thailand for passage to safety.

Raudsepp: Special thanks to my Aunt Marguerite Kelnhoffer and John McDonald for their many suggestions and assistance in editing. Also, special thanks to my parents, John and Rosalie, for their ongoing support and enthusiasm.

Our joint thanks to Erika MacKay for the use of her photographs—Angkor Wat with cow, Monks near Pond, taken on her trip to Cambodia, 1997.

Thanks to Edward Alec Genery (Teddy) for the artistic rendition of Tha, running from one camp to another in his escape (Front Cover of the Book). Aug 2023